W9-BPN-250

THE ENCYCLOPEDIA OF
MUSICAL INSTRUMENTS

PERCUSSION
& ELECTRONIC
INSTRUMENTS

Produced by Carlton Books Limited
20 Mortimer Street
London, W1N 7RD

Text and design copyright © Carlton Books Limited 2001

First published in hardback edition in 2001 by Chelsea House Publishers,
an imprint of Infobase Publishing. Printed and bound in Dubai.

9 8 7 6 5 4 3

The Chelsea House World Wide Web address is at http://www.chelseahouse.com

Library of Congress Cataloging-in-Publication Date applied for

Woodwind and Brass Instruments ISBN: 0-79106-091-8
Stringed Instruments ISBN: 0-79106-092-6
Percussion and Electronic Instruments ISBN: 0-79106-093-4
Keyboard Instruments and Ensembles ISBN: 0-79106-094-2
Non-Western and Obsolete Instruments ISBN: 0-79106-095-0

THE ENCYCLOPEDIA OF
MUSICAL INSTRUMENTS

PERCUSSION & ELECTRONIC INSTRUMENTS

ROBERT DEARLING

CHELSEA HOUSE
PUBLISHERS
An imprint of Infobase Publishing

THE ENCYCLOPEDIA OF
MUSICAL INSTRUMENTS

PERCUSSION & ELECTRONIC INSTRUMENTS

Woodwind and Brass Instruments

Stringed Instruments

Keyboard Instruments and Ensembles

Non-Western and Obsolete Instruments

CONTENTS

Percussion Instruments

Youthful concertgoers often find the percussion section of the orchestra immediately attractive. Strings, woodwind and brass offer mysteries yet to be solved, but with percussion you can instantly see what is happening. Furthermore, percussion makes fine sounds. The timpanist crouches over his drums, tapping them lightly and listening (making sure they are in tune, see page 10), then hitting them with exciting thwacks at the appointed times. The bass drummer will set pulses throbbing with the deep thud of his enormous drum, and in really colourful music the side drum, cymbals, triangle and perhaps even more exotic instruments, such as Chinese block, tom-tom, wind machine, castanets and whip, will add their stimulating sounds. With the crashing of metal on metal, metal on wood and wood on wood (and the presence of kettle drums), it was inevitable that the percussion instruments came to be known irreverently as 'the kitchen department'.

Left: marble relief from the Cantoria by Luca della Robbia, dated c. 1435, showing cherubs dancing to angels playing pipe and drums.

Percussion is probably the oldest of all the instrumental groups. It has been used to accompany dancing, ceremonies and battle since prehistoric days, whether it be wooden bowls or frames with membranes attached, bells, or blocks of wood or stone which ring when hit. Percussion actually means two bodies coming together forcibly. However, that is not the end of it. The two bodies might meet gently or be slid against one another, as is sometimes required of cymbals, and subtle effects can be created with light touches on tubular bells, tam–tam, triangle – in fact, almost any of the percussion instruments.

By convention, percussionists are also called upon to operate other instruments which fail to qualify as woodwind, brass or strings. While the xylophone is undoubtedly a struck instrument, the glockenspiel is less obviously so since one version of it has a keyboard and resembles a miniature piano – but then, the piano, for all its strings, is a percussion instrument itself, for its strings are hit by hammers.

With the wind machine (not a wind instrument!) the player turns a handle, which shows how versatile percussionists have to be. This is not meant slightingly. For all the apparent expenditure of muscle that it takes to play the drums, percussionists are a well-trained, disciplined and skilful group of performers. Without their skill the carefully written requirements of composers, who spend a great deal of thought upon obtaining the percussive sounds they want in their music, would descend to mere meaningless noise. |ᗷ

WORKS FOR
Percussion Alone

Only in the 1930s was it realized that diverse and entertaining sounds could be coaxed from a, by then, large range of percussion.

GEORGE ANTHEIL *Ballet Méchanique* (1924, revised 1954), for four pianolas, two xylophones, glockenspiel, timpani, tenor and bass drums, military drum, triangle, gong, cymbals, woodblock, aeroplane propellers (ie, recordings of aeroplane engines), and two electric bells. Originally written for an abstract film, and re-composed for concert performance, it represents, according to Antheil, "the barbaric and mystic splendour of modern civilization – mathematics of the universe in which the abstraction of the human soul lives."

BELA BARTOK Sonata for two pianos and percussion (1937). A fully–fledged recital work of amazing originality and imagination.

CARLOS CHAVEZ *Toccata* (1942), for xylophone, side drum, Indian drums, tenor and bass drums, bells, cymbals (suspended), large and small gongs, chimes, claves and maracas. A work of mesmeric rhythms, constantly changing in detail but maintaining a fascinating momentum.

HENRY COWELL *Ostinato Pianissimo* (1934), for four percussionists, who maintain, as the work's title suggests, a quiet rhythm throughout. *Pulse* (1939), for brake drums, pipe lengths, dubaci, rice bowls, woodblocks, dragons' mouths, tom-toms, drums, cymbals and gongs. An extraordinary rhythmic exercise in constantly varying timbres.

SIEGFRIED FINK *Beat the Beat*, for bass drum, two tom-toms, snare drum, hi-hat, cymbals and cow bells. Intended for a solo beat drummer, but written out rather than left to imagination.

ALAN HOVHANESS *October Mountain* (1942), for marimba, glockenspiel, timpani, tenor and bass drums, gong and tam–tam.

Marimba and glockenspiel provide the melodies, the rest create a mysterious atmosphere.

OSVALDO LACERDA *Three Brazilian Miniatures*, for vibraphone, timpani, side drum, xylophone and native Brazilian instruments.

RONALD LOPRESTI *Sketch* (1956), for xylophone, marimba, celeste, timpani, side drum, bass drum, gong, piano, triangle and cymbal (suspended), winner in 1956 of the first prize at the Eastman School of Music annual contest.

TORBJORN IWAN LUNDQUIST *Sisu* (1976), for xylophone, crotales, vibraphone, cymbals, marimba, tom-toms, xylorimba, tam–tam, timpani, Thai and Chinese gongs and tubular bells. This Swedish composer has a superbly subtle sense of rhythm and outstanding control of large forces.

ISTVAN MARTA *Doll's House Story* (1985), for percussion and synthesizer. A work of considerable length which tellingly blends natural drum sounds with synthetic gong chimes, marimbas, Chinese cymbals and bells.

LASZLO SARY *Pebble Playing in a Pot* (1978), in which marimbas somewhat over–insistently imitate the scene suggested in the title.

YOSHIHISA TAIRA *Hiérophonie V* (1974), for four timpani, six bongos, a small snare drum, eight gongs, two bass drums, two side drums, eight tom-toms, 16 woodblocks, eight claves, 15 Chinese woodblocks, whip, wood chimes, maracas, log drum, nine dubaci, five tam-tams, eight Thai gongs, four anvils, Chinese cymbal, eight Philippine gongs, three cow bells, flexatone, two glass chimes, six Turkish cymbals, two metal sheets, saw and Chinese gong. This Japanese composer draws on his nation's drumming tradition by encouraging his players to utter cries as they attack their instruments.

🎼 TIMPANI

TIMPANI, ALSO CALLED kettledrums because of the cauldron-like hemispherical shape of their bowls, are the kernel of the percussion group. Today, it is rare to encounter an orchestral work lacking timpani.

While 'kettle', from Latin *catillus* = small bowl, refers to the body of the instrument, the modern name, 'timpani' (singular: timpano), describes the head; this relates to tympanum, after the membrane in the eardrum. Orchestral timpani are tuned to definite pitches. At one time their heads were laboriously tensioned by laces, and later screws were used to apply tension where the outer rim of the skin is connected to the body. In practice, this meant that once the drum had been tuned it could sound only that note until it was re-tuned. An alternative method of tuning in some drums is by rotating the bowls. Modern timpani are tuned by means of pedals, allowing instantaneous re-tuning and even the possibility of *glissandi*. Pedal timpani are called 'machine' drums.

🎼 Early History

Once Stone Age man had learnt to carve wood and cure animal skins, drums could be made. Hollowed-out logs, ceramic pots, perhaps even tortoise or turtle shells, were turned into drums with a calf-skin or other animal hide stretched across the top and fastened with a cord or a strip of leather. So ancient are these experiments that it is impossible to state categorically where timpani originated. The Middle East has given us the earliest representation of one, in a Babylonian plaque of about 700 BC. Thereafter, drawings and paintings including them are quite common. They show kettledrums ranging from very small to very large, and from shallow to deep, with the bowl shape varying from conical to rotund. These instruments were used in court for ceremonial purposes, less formally for danc-

🎼 THERE ARE FEW MORE MENIAL TASKS FOR A SERVANT THAN TO ACT AS A HUMAN DRUM SUPPORT, AS IN THIS EARLY 18TH-CENTURY TURKISH SCENE.

1565: The first known use of timpani in the orchestra occurred in a French *intermède* (a short interlude to provide contrast between sections of a larger work) titled *Psyche ed Amore* (composer unknown).

1607: It is probable that their first operatic use was in Monteverdi's *Orfeo*, which opens with a magnificent Toccata for trumpets. The coupling of kettledrums with trumpets was common practice in the military for three centuries before Monteverdi's time, so as trumpets were playing on this occasion it is almost certain that drums would also have been in attendance. Even as late as the early 19th century, composers were still considering them almost as one voice.

1700 or before: The first symphony to include timpani was Giuseppe Torelli's Symphony in C, G33.

c. 1775: The first concerto for timpani was written by the Bohemian composer, oboist and timpanist Jiří Družecký, who scored it for oboe, eight timpani and orchestra. A symphony (formerly attributed to Hertel) by Johann Carl Christian Fischer is actually a concerto for eight timpani and orchestra. It dates from about 1782.

ing, and belligerently in war. By the 13th century in the Middle East mounted drummers came to be associated with mounted trumpeters, as indeed they did later in Europe where it became standard practice in concert halls, though by then the steeds had been dispensed with. Trumpets had been used occasionally without drums, especially in virtuoso roles, since the early 18th century, but in orchestral music trumpets and timpani were considered inseparable by composers, who often failed to indicate that the latter were required; it was 'understood'. Many drummers employed primarily for the court militia could not read music, and took their cues from the trumpeters.

If timpani became established first in the Middle East, they soon spread to India and Europe, where new varieties arose. Small hand-drum pairs, *tabla* and *bayan*, are now familiar in India: they are miniature kettledrums much more deserving of that name than the 'cauldron' drums of elsewhere. In Arabia, the *naqqara* were small kettledrums up to 25cm (10 inches) in skin

A TIMPANIST WITH A RANGE OF 'MACHINE' DRUMS (IE, WITH PEDALS FOR TUNING), AND AN EVEN LARGER RANGE OF STICKS FOR PERCUSSIVE EFFECTS.

diameter. They spread west and north; in England they are the ancestors of orchestral timpani and were called *nakers* (to rhyme with 'crackers'). Pronounced 'nackers' (not related to a knacker, a person who deals in old horses), this slang word has a musical, not a vulgar, origin. A player of two *nakers* would suspend them against his upper thighs from a waist belt. *Nakers* were useful for small parties of instrumentalists at court or in taverns; because they were portable they could be heard in almost any situation which demanded rhythm. They were of less use for formal gatherings.

By the time orchestras were first assembled (about 1600) to provide support for the singers in opera and oratorio, kettledrums had grown and developed a stronger voice. From there they moved with the rest of the orchestra into the

concert hall and by 1800 had become a permanent part of the orchestra. Of course, not all operas or concert works called for drums, though opera generally gained from their presence because they could reinforce dramatic moments, imitate thunder in wild weather scenes, herald the entrance of ominous characters, announce the arrival of important personages and so on. The demands on timpani increased. No longer were they required purely as 'noise-makers', so the problem of tuning had to be addressed.

TIMPANI EXPERIMENTS

ONE CAN IMAGINE the difficulties players encountered in the early days in trying to tune their kettledrums, and keep them in tune. Laces attached to the skins had to be tensioned with wooden chocks and brute force. Animal skins, perhaps inefficiently cured and dried, would slacken if hit too hard, and atmospheric humidity, or lack of it, made tuning to the correct pitch haphazard.

On the battlefield, if a soldier noticed that one of the cavalry's drums had gone out of tune he is likely to have had too many other things on his mind to let it worry him. There were two drums somewhere in the mêlée, one high pitched, the other low, and when they sounded a certain rhythm it would indicate 'advance', 'stand' or 'retreat', while a continuous high-pitched rattle would order 'left wheel', a

low-pitched one the opposite. That was all a soldier needed to know. Tone-deaf soldiers had to take their lead from comrades.

The situation was more critical in opera and concert performances. Laces were still in use in the 1730s, although by this time German drum makers had introduced screw tensioning. With this method, tuning is effected by turning screws at the rim of the skin: tightening the skin raised pitch, loosening it lowered pitch. Turning was achieved by means of a key or by a stick through loops or rings. Much trial and error was needed to obtain the right pitch and a great deal of care to avoid tearing the delicate vellum skin. Screw-

♪ A 'MACHINE' TIMPANO, THIS ONE PART OF THE BERLIN PHILHARMONIC ORCHESTRA'S 'KITCHEN DEPARTMENT', OFFERS QUICK, ACCURATE TUNING.

♪ A TIMPANIST REHEARSING UNDER HERMANN SCHERCHEN TESTS HIS INSTRUMENT'S TUNING BY TAPPING THE SKIN WITH THE FINGERTIPS.

tensioned timpani are still occasionally seen, mainly for historical accuracy in 'authentic performance' ensembles.

Some composers circumvented the problem of the time needed to change the note by the simple expedient of requiring more than the standard pair of timpani. Johann Melchior Molter wrote a Symphony in F (rather, a suite) about the middle of the 18th century which called for timpani tuned to five different notes, the effect in performance being almost that of a timpani continuo. Haydn dared not rely upon the availability of more than two timpani for his London concerts at the Hanover Square Rooms in 1791. The first movement of Symphony No. 94 in G, 'Surprise', requires timpani tuned to G and D with the G instrument having to retune to A. The composer neatly got round the problem by allowing the timpanist a full 19 bars to make the change from G to A – and a further 17 to retune back to G. His oratorio *The Creation* (1799) calls for seven re-tuning operations.

Clearly, drum makers were falling behind the requirements of composers. They responded with various inventions. In 1821 a rotating bowl was introduced in Amsterdam. A cable arrangement by a London maker included a pitch indicator which, so a famous timpanist recently remarked, "is less reliable than my ears". An early pedal timpano (1855) by saxophone-inventor Adolphe Sax proved to be a remarkable affair. The skin was extended taut over a cone-shaped resonator and pedals operated a series of shutters which blocked off certain lengths of the resonating tube, according to the note required. Rods, rings, cams, pedals and handles were all brought to bear on the problem, but none of these experiments found total success.

PROMINENT
Timpani
IN THE ORCHESTRA

One of the most startling timpani solos opens Bach's *Christmas Oratorio* (1734), answered immediately by flutes to create a pompous introduction to the chorus *Jauchet, frohlocket* ('Rejoice, exult').

JOSEPH HAYDN sometimes wrote adventurously for timpani, notably when it, and the rest of the orchestra, provides the surprise chord "to startle the ladies" in the Andante of the eponymous Symphony No. 94. However, a greater surprise comes in the finale, when a *forte* timpani entry abruptly follows eight quiet bars.

BEETHOVEN virtually liberated the timpani from its predominantly subordinate role, most dramatically in the Symphony No. 9, 'Choral' (1823). No less than 41 continuous bars of ferocious drumming mark the climax of the first movement's development, and solo timpani octaves, highly unusual in themselves at that date, answer the opening string phrases of the Scherzo.

Thereafter, timpani were used with increasing freedom and increasing dramatic effect, as in Tchaikovsky's *Romeo and Juliet Overture* (1880), a doom-laden crescendo near the end, and in the first movement of Dvořák's Symphony No. 9, *From the New World* (1893), where they decisively confirm the first *tutti* in the first movement and make exciting contributions later in the work.

Paralleling Beethoven a century later, Stravinsky set percussion totally free. His *Rite of Spring* (1913) requires incredible virtuosity from the timpanists as well as from the rest of the large orchestra. Three years later Carl Nielsen's Symphony No. 4, 'The Inextinguishable', placed a timpanist on either side of the orchestra and in conflict with it, maintaining, according to the composer's instructions, a menacing tone throughout.

Since then, Holst, Bartók, Britten, Tubin and many others have utilized the wide possibilities offered by modern pedal timpani. Some, such as the Belgian Victor Legley and the New Zealander Lyell Cresswell, have provided concertos for timpani and orchestra.

Finally, during the early years of the 20th century, a wholly satisfactory pedal system was introduced whereby, with the player seated, foot pressure controlled the pitch of the drum. Sophisticated models gave the timpanist the facility of a tuning gauge. But even with this refinement, in passages where different timpani notes occur in quick succession, one drum is still required for each note.

A TURKISH KETTLE-DRUM PLAYER OF THE EARLY 18TH CENTURY.

MULTIPLE TIMPANI

A PAIR OF TIMPANI were required by most composers until about 1800. Various tunings were called for but things settled down to one drum tuned to the tonic (the key the work was 'in') and another tuned a fourth below. Therefore, in a work in C major, one drum would be tuned to C,

A SELECTION OF DRUM STICKS WITH HEADS RANGING FROM SPONGE AND WOOD TO IVORY AND WIRE.

the other to the G below. This meant that, in sonata-form movements in C major, when the second theme arrived in the dominant, five steps up the scale (ie, G major), the lower drum was now in the new 'tonic'. However, when the slow movement arrived, usually in the subdominant (F major in our C major example) either the timpani had to be retuned or stay silent. Mostly, they stayed silent.

As we have seen, some composers introduced additional timpani to deal with such tonal problems, but this did not become acceptable practice until the middle of the 19th century. Before then, Antonín Reicha, an experimenter with many musical

novelties to his credit, required eight timpani in *Abschied der Johanna d'Arc* (1806), a score which, incidentally, also includes the use of musical glasses. The rest of the 19th century saw a gradual and spasmodic use of multiple timpani, usually for special effects, but the bulk of standard works – Schumann, Brahms, even Nielsen (only later would he fully exploit the possibilities of percussion) – use the traditional pair. In *The Planets* suite (1914–16) Gustav Holst wrote for two timpanists at six drums; almost a century earlier Berlioz had required 16 in his *Requiem* (1837).

Numerical superiority is not the only way to ensure percussive novelties in timpani writing. In 1794 the German composer Johann Paul Aegidius Martini, called Martini il Tedesco (Martini the German) – to distinguish him from several Italian Martinis around at the time, just in case his given names failed to do so – conceived the idea of striking two timpani of different pitches simultaneously in his opera *Sappho*. This idea appealed also to Stravinsky: he required five differently tuned timpani to be struck together in his *Rite of Spring* (1913). A variation of this, the hitting of one drum with two sticks, was adopted by Mahler in his Symphony No. 8 (1906).

ৎ Heads and Sticks

As indicated earlier, timpani skins were made of vellum (that is, calf skin) or sometimes skins of other bovines, such as ox. After World War II, however, the increasing availability of synthetic materials invaded the musical instrument business and plastic drum heads were introduced. Drummers still disagree as to whether this move resulted in a genuine advance in tonal quality. Drumsticks are made of wood but the ends, the part that makes contact with the skin, might be fashioned from a wide selection of materials and also vary greatly in shape.

Until recently, the sound of drums in performances of orchestral music was regarded as almost obscene. This attitude was partly a by-product of the 19th-century audience's insistence upon a 'heavy' wash of orchestral sound. A Bruckner pedal point on timpani had to be a distant murmur, and on no account should a single stroke be allowed to disturb the enveloping cloak of the rest of the orchestra. Anything as coarse as an identifiable drum stroke was frowned upon. It was almost as if drummers were present in the orchestra merely to be seen at their acrobatic antics, and not heard. This situation

was exacerbated by the inadequacies of early recording techniques. The grooves of 78rpm and LP discs were too violently distorted to enable accurate tracking of the pick-up by the abrupt impact of a drum attack. Drum noise had to be damped down almost to inaudibility, lest it upset the balance or the comfort of armchair listening.

Fortunately, tastes change and recording technology has come on apace. Listeners now like to hear the voices of the drums. Drumsticks might be made of two layers of felt over a hard core, giving a smooth, rounded tone, or hard felt or wood, which produce a sharp and incisive sound. There are grades between these extremes, and the shape of the head also varies from spherical to wheel-shaped, via oval and pear-shaped. The correct stick is now chosen to suit the music being played. Sticks are held between thumbs and the first two fingers, and there is usually a ferrule of wood, plastic or metal to aid grip.

HECTOR BERLIOZ IN 1846, THE YEAR HE COMPLETED *THE DAMNATION OF FAUST*. HIS PREDILECTION FOR LARGE FORCES EXTENDED TO A GENEROUS PERCUSSION CONTINGENT.

UNUSUAL USES OF *Timpani*

Apart from unusual tunings, which were adopted by many composers for specific effects or purposes, imaginative deployment of orchestral timpani began, possibly, in 1781, when Mozart called for them to be muted (ie, covered with a cloth) in the opera *Idomeneo*. Haydn required the same in Symphony No. 102 in B flat (1794). Berlioz, in his *Symphonie fantastique* (1830), marked his timpani part *baguettes d'eponge* ('with sponge-headed sticks') to create approaching thunder in the third movement and a feeling of dread in the following 'March to the Guillotine'. Later in that fourth movement, a fearsome rattle is created at the direction *baguette de bois* ('with wooden sticks').

In 1899 Elgar directed that a timpani roll in the *Enigma* Variations should be executed with side drum sticks to suggest the engine of an ocean liner, but he later agreed that two coins tapping the skins would equal the effect. Charles Villiers Stanford asked for timpani to be played with fingertips in *Song of the Fleet* (1910), and both Nielsen in Symphony No. 2, *The Four Temperaments* (1902), and Britten, in the opera *Death in Venice* (1973), instructed that drumsticks be laid aside and the timpani played with birch twigs.

♪ SIDE·DRUM

SIDE DRUMS ARE frame drums, with a circular wood or metal frame and two heads of parchment. Usually the frame is shallower than the diameter of the heads (an exception is the long drum), and a snare is fitted against the outside of the lower (or upper) head. This snare, which gives the instrument its alternative name of snare drum (one preferred in jazz and popular music circles), consists of wires of gut in older models or, lately, nylon. When the upper head of the drum is struck with hard sticks the vibration within the drum is carried to the lower head where the snares react by rattling against the skin, producing a sharp hissing sound. This, combined with the instrument's naturally high tone, results in a distinctive noise that can cut through the heaviest orchestration. In certain circumstances the snares can be released from the head to give a tone not unlike that of a tom-tom.

In older models of side drum the skins were tensioned by ropes in a 'V' configuration with thongs which, when slid upwards, converted the 'V' into a 'Y', thereby increasing the tension. In modern orchestral side drums the tension is achieved by metal rods. Side drums are not tuned to a specific pitch: it is up to the player and/or conductor to decide what is the most effective tensioning for the work to be played.

Sticks are made of wood, with a plastic or ivory striking head in the form of a slim acorn. Typically, sticks measure about 40cm (16 inches). The drum bodies reach a maximum of 30cm (12 inches) deep, and the parchment (or plastic) heads a maximum of 40cm in diameter. Older models of both drums and drum sticks vary widely. Some drums resembled large barrels, which must have been tiring to carry if suspended round the neck or from a belt, and drumsticks ranged in shape from small clubs to unadorned wooden sticks.

♪ Early History

As with all drums, the side drum's origin is lost in antiquity. Small drums of all shapes and sizes existed thousands of years ago, many of them shallow framed such as are encountered even now in non-orchestral environments in many countries. One of the earliest representations of snares is to be found on a relief dated about 1454

♪ A PROVENÇAL LONG SIDE DRUM WITH
SNARES AGAINST THE UPPER FACE.
THE DRUMMER ALSO OPERATES A
RECORDER.

♪ A MID-18TH CENTURY SIDE
DRUM AND DRUM STICKS.
AGAIN, THE SNARE OF THE
DRUM LIES ACROSS THE UPPER
SKIN.

in the church of St. Francis at Rimini. The drum is held perpendicularly from its frame by a cord in the left hand. A snare lies against the head, which is being beaten.

The side drum was originally used in military establishments, and that is where it got its name. Slung by a cord round the soldier's neck, the instrument hung against his side with the head at an angle. Its distinctive voice could be heard at considerable distances by marching men and in the heat of battle. The tradition, now he struck with a stick in the right hand.

Side drums play a vital part in military ceremonies of the British Army. In Scottish Highland regiments, for example, the drummers are tasked with setting up rhythmic patterns for the bagpipes. This requires immense skill and discipline. The drums set the tempo of the march at the start and maintain the pace when the pipers pause for breath or between tunes. As with military timpani, the side drum was also once used to pass messages and give instructions in the battlefield and in camp. It once served to accompany ceremonial floggings in the navy, adding a spurious solemnity to a barbarous act.

dying out, of military drummers donning leopard skins over their uniforms began in the late 18th century, when a fashion for black drummers arose. Military bands for long maintained this exotic symbol as a reminder of the past.

℅ In Performance

Side drums, it was once maintained, are most effective when performing rolls or repeated quasi-military rhythms. This may have been true in the days of luxurious orchestrations, but now, with leaner sounds and the increasing incidence of chamber sonorities even in works for full orchestra, composers are quite happy to write

DRUMMERS OF THE ARGYLE AND SUTHERLAND HIGHLANDERS, COMPLETE IN THEIR FULL CEREMONIAL REGALIA WITH LEOPARD SKINS.

single notes and intricate rhythms, knowing that the drums will make their due effect.

Side drums have been put to a number of musical purposes. In Elizabethan England and elsewhere the combination of pipe and tabor, to accompany dancing or marching, was common among travelling musicians. The tabor needed only to have one or more snares – as on occasion they did – to qualify as a snare drum. The musician would have a flageolet in the left hand and a small tabor hung from the neck or waist which

Side Drum
TERMINOLOGY
℅

BATTER HEAD The upper playing skin; that which is 'battered'.

DRAG A roll.

FLAM A two-note figure.

MAMMY-DADDY The technique of producing a roll on the side drum, each stick alternately striking twice in quick succession to make a seamless roll.

PARRADIDDLE A descriptive way of indicating a succession of strokes: single, flam, drag.

RIM SHOT The laying of one stick on the drum head and rim simultaneously while this stick is struck with the other to make a very loud *staccato* sound, similar to a pistol shot.

RUFF A short series of quick notes terminating in a *forte* stroke.

SNARE The wires running under the lower head which vibrate against the head when the upper skin is struck.

SNARE HEAD The lower head, against which the snares lie.

SIDE DRUMS IN PERFORMANCE

MOST OF US ARE used to seeing the side drum as a member of the orchestral percussion. The French composer Marin Marais was apparently the first to use it in this role, possibly in his opera *Alcione* (1706). Far easier to verify is Handel's call for side drums in his *Musick for the Royal Fireworks* (1749). André-Ernest-Modeste Grétry was the first to use a side drum in a symphony: his multi-movement overture (a symphony in all but name) to the opera *Le Magnifique* (1773). The instrument's first appearance in a true symphony is courtesy of the little-known Bohemian composer František Krystof Neubauer, who includes *tamburo*, by which is meant side drum, in his highly

descriptive 'Battle' Symphony, Op. 11. This work commemorates the so-called 'Siege of Helden Coburg', when Field Marshal Prince Coburg-Saalfeld led his Austrian army to victory over the Turks at Martinesti, Romania, on 22 September 1789. Mozart marked the same event that year with a lightweight country dance notable for

RIGHT: CLASSICAL PERCUSSIONIST JAMES BLADES IN ACTION. BELOW: A MODERN SET OF 'TRAPS' FOR JAZZ AND ROCK USE. THE HI-HAT CYMBALS AND BASS DRUM ARE FOOT-OPERATED.

its exclusion of all military instruments.

Neubauer's remarkable work predates Beethoven's notorious 'Battle' Symphony by 24 years. Beethoven gave the opposing French and English armies their own side drum signals in his 'recreation' of the Battle of Vitoria, but sadly omitted the ingredient of genius. Rossini gave side drums unusual solo status at the start of his *Thieving Magpie* Overture (1817). Most famous of all in the side drum's repertoire is the gruelling slow crescendo of Ravel's *Boléro* in which, for over 300 bars, side drummers have to repeat the same rhythm while gradually increasing the power of the tone. Shostakovich combined Ravel's idea with vivid images of war in his 'Leningrad' Symphony (1941). In the first movement the approaching German army is represented by a two-bar pattern played no fewer than 176 times by side drum, rising from *ppp* to *fff*, and later a further ten times, fading to silence. Even if shared between players, this slow build-up of tension must rank as one of the most arduous of all side drum parts for the endurance, concentration and sheer physical strength required for its performance.

Various methods of making the side drum 'speak' in unusual ways have been devised by composers. The American Aaron Copland, in his Symphony No. 3 (1946), employs a most telling example of rim shot (see page 15). His compatriot William Russell's *Fugue for Eight Percussion Instruments* shows even greater imagination: at one point a piece of paper is placed over the drum head; at another, a handkerchief; and a resined glove or cloth is to be rubbed over the drum stick. Incidentally, Russell extended his oblique requirements to the piano, whose strings have to be played *pizzicato* with fingertips and fingernails, and scratched lengthways with a coin. Conventional use of the side drum in an unconventional setting is met in a Piano Sonata (1927) by the Russo-American composer Nikolai Lopatnikov, wherein it is awarded an important part.

Nielsen
AND THE SIDE DRUM

Early audiences at performances of Carl Nielsen's Symphony No. 5 (1922) were at first puzzled, then alarmed and finally driven in terror from the hall by the anarchic behaviour of the side drummer. It was indeed an extraordinary scene. The man seemed to go crazy. He stood near the back of the orchestra and created such a frenzy of noise that the orchestra, playing at full blast, was almost overwhelmed. What did it mean?

DANISH COMPOSER CARL NIELSEN'S IMAGINATIVE EMPLOYMENT OF PERCUSSION SENT AUDIENCES HURRYING TO THE EXIT.

It was Nielsen's instruction to him that had caused him to display this behaviour. He must "improvise as if at all costs to stop the progress of the orchestra". This was not some modern gimmick to create headlines but a scrupulously planned strategy to convey the message of Nielsen's latest work. In his depiction of good versus evil, the composer divided his instrumental forces into two opposing camps, with the side drum (together with the clarinet, cymbals, triangle, etc.) given the role of an evil 'character'. The majority of the orchestra represented 'good'. A well-worn cliché, perhaps, but superbly carried out.

The symphony opens negatively, then disruptive figures are quietly introduced. These coalesce into a frightening march led by a repetitive side drum rhythm. Eventually this episode fades and yields to a noble Adagio ('the forces of good') which also fades, only to return. At this return it is attacked by the disruptive elements and a battle ensues. At its height, the side drum re-enters and launches upon its 'death or glory' assault. No two side drummers play the same music here, this being an improvisation. Some are not equal to being 'evil'; others let go with enormous vehemence, introducing every kind of alien rhythm and letting off 'rim shots' as the crisis approaches. Side drummers can show distinct signs of fatigue after their ordeal, even expressing regret at their failure to stop the orchestra.

Six years later Nielsen returned to the side drum, in his Clarinet Concerto. Written with the clarinettist of the Copenhagen Wind Quintet, Aage Oxenvad, in mind, this work reflects Nielsen's interest in the make-up of his fellow men. Oxenvad is characterized (accurately) as a sharp-tempered, choleric but humorous and at base kindly man. Nielsen adds a biting edge to the character in a carefully written and elaborate part for the side drum, which at times 'argues', at others 'agrees', with the clarinet. Unlike the symphony, open conflict is avoided, but familiarity with both works points up the strong link between them. Furthermore, both works allow the side drum more freedom and prominence than others in the repertoire.

♭ BASS DRUM

VISUALLY, THE BASS DRUM is an imposing instrument. It cannot be overlooked as it stands vertically in the percussion section (see pages 16 and 21). Some models are mounted on a stand (see page 20) to enable alteration of the head angle, especially for works that demand that the percussionists move quickly from instrument to instrument. Like the side drum, the bass drum is an instrument of indefinite pitch, which means it does not need to be tuned to a definite note. Its voice can change according to what the composer requires of it, from the slightest mutter to an elemental thundercrack. The instrument is equally effective at producing single notes or rolls.

The modern bass drum has two plastic heads, each with a skin diameter of approximately one metre; the depth of the wooden frame is about half this. A single-headed variety, of vellum, with a shallower frame was once quite common. This type was called the gong drum, due to its appearance not its material. Since their invention almost 6000 years ago, large drums have tended to reduce in size for standard usage, though there are exceptions (see below). Early versions stood nearly 2m (7 feet) high and were installed in permanent positions in court or palace, probably as a rallying point or time signal. Bass drums were known in Asia by at least 3500BC, and some thousand years later they were part of Sumerian culture. They have since appeared in many different forms.

♭ MINSTRELS AT VAUXHALL GARDENS, IN 1806, WITH TURKISH PERCUSSION (CYMBALS, TRIANGLE, BASS DRUM, TURKISH CRESCENT, TAMBOURINE) AND PANPIPES.

✶ *The Bass Drum and Janissary Music*

The modern orchestral bass drum is clearly descended from a Turkish military model, the 14th century *davul*, which is approximately the same size and in the same proportions. The *davul* has two heads, but is laced as opposed to being screw-tensioned, and struck with a heavy wooden beater rather than the large felt-headed drumsticks commonly used by orchestral drummers. During the heyday of the Ottoman empire in the late 14th century the peoples of the Balkans came to fear the sounds associated with the Turkish armies. Principal among these was the noise created by the *davul*, together with shawms, jingles and cymbals, which signalled the

approach of the invaders. The Sultan's guard was made up of 'new troops' (*yeni çeri*), or Janissaries (war captives who were trained into an elite fighting corps). Their war-like sound was thus termed 'Janissary music'. Although other instruments were included, the combination of cymbals, jingles and bass drum came to be so closely identified with this music that 18th-century composers, wishing to add exotic Eastern colour to their Turkish opera plots or concert pieces, invariably scored for them, replacing the jingles with a triangle.

In a military band the soldier playing the big drum has it strapped vertically in front of him, striking it with the drumstick held in the left hand while the right hand damps the reverberation of the skin on the opposite side. To the bystanders' amusement, the drummer's right hand jumps away from the skin and back again at every blow. Unlike the orchestral bass drum, which is rod-tensioned, military models still adhere to rope-tensioning, in which ropes are attached criss-cross between the heads and tightened by sliding braces.

An interesting variation arose in the military use of the bass drum and came about in imitation of Janissary music. In cases where the drum possesses two heads, one would sometimes be played with a cane or birch twig, and these might even be used on the drum casing. In his 'Military' Symphony, No. 100, Haydn faithfully reflected this practice (which is more than most performances manage) by writing the bass drum part on one line with the note tails descending for normal strokes and ascending for the birch twig strikes. The downbeats are accented by the drumstick strikes. Birch twigs on the skin produce a dry, flat sound with a faint resonance, but when beaten on the drum casing this resonance is further reduced and the result merely provides rhythmic pulse.

So pervasive did this Turkish craze become in the 18th century that it even entered music whose scoring is totally devoid of percussion. Mozart, in the finale of his Violin Concerto No. 5 in A, K219 (1775), known as the 'Turkish', switched to A minor for an extended episode strongly redolent of folk music of that culture. About eight years later another A major work

𝄞 BASS DRUMMERS USING HEADLESS STICKS AND LEADING A SOMEWHAT DEPLETED PROCESSION; NORTH OF ENGLAND, 1930S.

JANISSARY *Percussion* IN OPERA AND CONCERT

The description 'Janissary music' indicates exotic music, often in A minor, which is intended to convey the flavour of Turkish military bands with cymbals, triangle (substituting for Turkish crescent) and bass drum. The following works may all be described as 'Janissary music':

GIOVANNI DOMENICO FRESCHI *Berenice vendicativa*, opera (1680).

GOTTFRIED FINGER *Concerto alla turchesa* (c. 1725).

CHRISTOPH WILLIBALD GLUCK *Le cadi dupé*, opera (1761); *La rencontre imprévue*, opera (1764); *The Pilgrims of Mecca*, opera (1764).

GEORG GLANTZ 'Turkish' Symphony (1774).

JOHANN MICHAEL HAYDN 'Turkish' Suite from music to Voltaire's *Zaire* (1777); Turkish March in C (1795).

WOLFGANG AMADEUS MOZART *Die Entführung aus dem Serail* (opera) (1782).

FRANZ JOSEPH HAYDN Symphony No 100 in G, 'Military' (1794).

LUDWIG VAN BEETHOVEN 'The Ruins of Athens' (incidental music) (1812), 'Battle' Symphony (1813'), Symphony No 9 in D minor, 'Choral', (1823).

put the whole of the finale into A minor. This is the Piano Sonata in A, K331, where the finale is marked *Allegretto alla turka* and popularly called the 'Turkish rondo'. Some pianos of the time were equipped with percussive attachments that not only rang little bells to imitate the Turkish crescent but also damped the lower strings to create the impression of a bass drum. 𝄢

BASS DRUM IN THE ORCHESTRA

IN THE 17TH CENTURY the bass drum was waiting to be introduced into the orchestra. People were already familiar with big drums in the spheres of folk and ethnic music. As so often, it was via the opera house that this novelty came to be accepted in a serious work, in 1680 (see panel). Its acceptance grew quite gradually during the next century and a half, being carried by the Janissary connection (see page 18–19). Then came Berlioz.

If Haydn, followed by Beethoven, liberated the timpani, Berlioz released the bass drum from its association with Turkey. Within three years of

Beethoven's 'Choral' Symphony, Berlioz had scored for bass drum in his very first orchestral work, the Overture *Les francs juges*, omitting cymbals and triangle. Part of the drum's function was to reinforce the cross-rhythm of the timpani in the central section. Later, in his *Grande messe des morts*, Berlioz required the drum's two skins to be struck alternately with padded sticks.

Thereafter, the bass drum was used frequently by many composers and with increasing imagination, its Turkish adjuncts rarely if ever in attendance. Liszt is credited as the first to require a bass drum roll, in his first symphonic poem, *Ce qu'on entend sur la montagne*, though the idea may have come from Joachim Raff who assisted Liszt with orchestration in his early works. An effective roll in Dukas's *Sorcerer's Apprentice* is created by twisting a double-headed stick to produce rapid strokes, an effect taken up by Stravinsky in *The Firebird*.

But a problem remained: audibility. Heavy orchestration can smother the bass drum's natural tone unless some means can be found to accentuate it. Composers have found different solutions to this shortcoming. In his *Missa da Requiem* Verdi called for a 'very large bass drum'; in *En Saga* Sibelius required the extra clarity imparted by the use of timpani sticks; and in *Madama Butterfly* Puccini instructed that the instrument be attacked with an iron rod. In Britten's opera *Peter Grimes* the bass drum is

A MODERN BASS DRUM BY YAMAHA, MOUNTED ON A SWIVELLING FRAME FOR 'FACE TO FACE' PLAYING.

struck with side drum sticks. And, in a revision to his original score to *The Rite of Spring*, Stravinsky asked for wooden sticks to be played near the edge of the skin.

Owing to its spare and cunning orchestration, Prokofiev's score for *Lieutenant Kijé* requires no such 'extras' to allow the bass drum to be heard. Shostakovich, too, realized the importance of lean scoring if the bass drum's voice is to be heard with clarity. He went to the extreme in his Cello Concerto No. 2, first movement, giving the bass drum eight *ff secco* ('very loud and dry') and five *mf* (medium loud) strokes, its only competition being from the cadenza of the soloist. In his Symphony No. 12, 'dedicated to the memory of Lenin', Shostakovich called for a strange percussive effect at the end of the first movement and leading into the second. Over the space of 95 bars he has the bass drum, side drum and timpani in unison, intermittently contributing to a vast *diminuendo*, opening at a violently hammering *fff* (extremely loud), dropping quickly and eventually reaching a whispered *morendo* (dying away). The effect of all three drum timbres together is both ominous and mysterious.

✄ Sizes

There is little doubt that drums, and particularly big drums, hold a fascination for audiences, whether at a concert or anywhere else. Showmen will attract a fairground or circus crowd to their displays by banging a drum (if, that is, they have resisted the temptation to modernize the process by deafening their prospective clients with a

THE PERCUSSION SECTION OF THE HALLÉ ORCHESTRA AT THE ROYAL FESTIVAL HALL, LONDON, IN 1952, A YEAR AFTER THE HALL OPENED TO THE PUBLIC.

ghetto-blaster), and the bigger the drum the better. Theoretically.

In practice there is a size at which a drum becomes dangerous because the vibrations within could cause it to explode if struck too enthusiastically. This size may almost have been reached by the Remo company of North Hollywood, California when, in 1961, they built a huge drum for Disneyland. Its head measures almost 3.7m (10.5 feet) in diameter and the instrument weighs 204kg (93lb). Such an instrument might have indulged the craze for large-scale effect displayed by Verdi, but practicalities preclude its use even for 'authentic' performance.

IMPORTANT WORKS IN THE
Bass drum's
HISTORY

BERLIOZ *Les francs juges*, Op. 3, overture (1826), the first orchestral work to use the bass drum independently of other Turkish percussion.

BRITTEN *Peter Grimes* (opera) (1945), uses side drum sticks; *Young Person's Guide to the Orchestra* (1946), a short solo with two drum rolls.

DUKAS *The Sorcerer's Apprentice*, scherzo (1897), includes rapid beats created with a double-headed drumstick.

LISZT *Ce qu'on entend sur la montagne*, symphonic poem (1849), believed to be the first use of the bass drum roll.

PROKOFIEV *Lieutenant Kijé*, suite from an aborted film (1934), gives prominent bass drum solo against light scoring.

PUCCINI *Madama Butterfly* (opera) (1904), requires an iron bar to replace the usual drumstick.

SHOSTAKOVICH Symphony No 12, Op. 112, 'The Year 1917' (1961), uses bass drum in unison with side drum and timpani; Cello Concerto No. 2, Op. 126 (1966), has bass drum strokes to accompany the cello cadenza.

SIBELIUS *En Saga*, symphonic poem (1892), uses timpani sticks.

STRAVINSKY *The Firebird* (ballet) (1910), as Dukas, above; *The Rite of Spring* (ballet) (revised version, 1947), calls for wooden sticks to be used near the edge of the skin.

VERDI *Missa da Requiem* (1874), requires the largest big drum available.

A-Z OF OTHER PERCUSSION

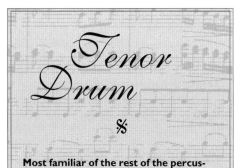

Tenor Drum

%

Most familiar of the rest of the percussion section is the tenor drum, also called the long drum. This type has a dry, commanding tone of no definite pitch, like that of a deep side drum without snares, although of decisive effect. Its use in the military in Europe was, and is, widespread, and it was from the military that it first ventured into the orchestra, where it has been employed by many 20th-century composers. Like so many other 'exotic' instruments, the tenor drum was given its first opportunity in 'serious' music by opera. Meyerbeer's grand opera *Robert le Diable* was a great success in Paris in 1831; its use of tenor drum probably suggested to Berlioz that the hollow voice of the instrument was appropriate for solemn, sacred music (two tenor drums occur in the *Grande Messe des morts* of 1837) and in a hymn of praise (his *Te Deum* of 1849 requires six tenor drums). At that time the instrument was tensioned by ropes. Modern examples use rods, as does the side drum. It may be struck with hard or soft sticks, depending upon the musical circumstances.

AFTER THE DRUMS, the percussion group boasts a whole host of varied instruments, some tuned to specific scales or notes, others not. The instruments listed below are of indefinite pitch (ie, they are untuned) unless otherwise noted.

% Castanets

A name taken from the Spanish for 'chestnuts' and the instrument itself taken from Spanish folk culture and chestnut wood. Castanets were in existence in Roman times and probably long before. Each castanet is a disc-shaped piece of wood, hollowed on one side and with flanges extended from the edge to hold the cord by which it and its fellow are held by the fingers. Traditionally the two discs are brought together rhythmically by manual manipulation, but this Spanish folk skill is rarely shared by orchestral musicians. They cheat by fastening the instruments to a piece of wood, upon which they are held apart by elastic until fingers play upon them. Naturally, non-Spanish composers wishing to evoke a Spanish atmosphere will employ castanets. The first to do so was Bizet in *Carmen* (1875), to be followed by Chabrier in *España*

(1883) and Massenet in his opera *Le Cid* (1885). In 1877 Saint-Saëns extended the geographical possibility of castanets by including them in *Samson and Delilah*, set in Gaza.

% Celeste

A 'heavenly' sounding instrument of definite pitch, invented in 1880 in Paris. Tchaikovsky, amid great secrecy, endeavoured to be the first to use this instrument of hammered metal plates in his *Nutcracker* ballet (1892), but he was thwarted by Charles Widor, who introduced it in his ballet *La Korrigane* (1880).

% Claves

Simply two sticks up to 25cm (10 inches) in length, struck together to provide a rhythmic accompaniment. Edgard Varèse was the first to use claves in his *Ionisation* (1931), and others have followed. Elisabeth Lutyens, the English composer, brought them into her curiously titled charade in four scenes and three interruptions, *Time off? – Not a Ghost of a Chance!*.

TENOR DRUMS BY PREMIER – HIGH-PITCHED AND SPECIALLY STRENGTHENED INSTRUMENTS FOR MARCHING.

22

ABOVE: EVELYN GLENNIE PLAYING HAND DRUMS. THIS BRILLIANT SCOTTISH PERCUSSIONIST COMPOSES AS WELL AS PLAYS.
BELOW RIGHT: THE SAFRI DUO.

𝄋 Cymbals

Of great antiquity, these are part of the Janissary music we met with under Bass Drum. China, so obviously the land of clashing metal, is probably innocent of cymbals; their place of origin may be Turkey or India. The design of these two plates banged together has undergone many detail changes. In shape they vary from slightly dished to cup-shaped; in size they can reach 65cm (26 inches) in diameter or be tiny enough to be held by threads to the finger and thumb of a dancer, to be sounded during the dance. The first use in serious music seems to have been in 1680, when Adam Strungk included them in his opera *Esther*. Since then they have done prominent service in many a 19th-century overture, and more recently have been sounded with a violin bow when suspended, and struck with beaters. 𝄡

Percussion
PERFORMERS
𝄋

AMADINDA PERCUSSION GROUP, a Hungarian ensemble formed in 1984 by Károly Bojtos, Zoltán Rácz, Zsolt Sárkány and Zoltán Váczi.

JAMES BLADES, though not a regular recitalist, is a world-renowned player with the London Symphony Orchestra (since 1940) and many other organizations. He is an unequalled percussion authority, giving lectures and broadcasts as well as making an illustrated recording about percussion in 1973 (see page 16).

ENSEMBLE BASH, formed in 1990 by Richard Benjafield, Stephen Hiscock, Chris Brannick and Andrew Martin. It is currently Britain's only professional percussion group.

EVELYN GLENNIE (left), Scottish percussion virtuoso and composer who, despite being deaf, recognizes the musical sounds through vibrations in her body and through her acute visual sense.

KODO, a Japanese group whose name means 'heart beat', founded in 1971 by Den Tagayasu. Originally called Ondekoza ('demon drum group'), the ensemble now consists of ten members who value, and maintain, traditional Japanese music.

KROUMATA PERCUSSION ENSEMBLE, formed in Stockholm by Ingvar Hallgren, Jan Hellgren, Anders Holdar, Anders Loguin and Martin Steisner. *Kroumata* is the ancient Greek generic term for percussion.

NEXUS, a Canadian ensemble formed in 1970 by Russell Hartenberger, John Wyre, Robin Engelman, Bob Becker and William Cahn. The group's repertoire ranges from ragtime to classical.

SAFRI DUO (shown below) Danish percussionists Uffo Savery and Martin Friis have played percussion together since, as children in the early 1970s, they joined the Tivoli Boys' Guard in Copenhagen. They arrange old music for percussion and work with contemporary composers during the writing of new works.

STRASBOURG PERCUSSION ENSEMBLE (Les Percussions de Strasbourg) was founded in that city in 1961 and has been conducted by, among others, Pierre Boulez.

JAMES WOOD, English composer and percussionist, and authority on percussion.

✄ Flexatone

Once described as the instrument with the least attractive sound of all (by a critic evidently unfamiliar with the serpent), the flexatone was invented in England in 1922. Two wooden knobs on wires flank a metal strip and when the instrument is shaken the knobs hit the strip to produce a rapid rattling sound. Meanwhile, the strip is capable of being flexed to change its note, and while this is happening a weird *glissando* effect is punctuated by the rattle. Honegger gave the flexatone its first chance in *Antigone* (1927), Khachaturian risked a solo for it in his Piano Concerto (1946), and the Finnish composer Lief Segerstam created symphonic history by putting one in his Symphony No. 11 (1986).

✄ Glockenspiel

(German for 'bell-play') An instrument of definite pitch, being a series of metal bars struck either directly with beaters or via a keyboard. Handel's call for 'carillon' in his oratorio *Saul*

WOMAN AND CHILD PLAYING A LARGE TAMBOURINE WHILE A SOLDIER PLAYS A PIPE; ENGLAND, C. 1780.

(1738) has been put forward as the earliest use of a *glockenspiel*, but as he is more likely to have used a frame of bells, the *glockenspiel* in Mozart's *The Magic Flute* (1791) is probably its earliest appearance. The Austrian-born Finnish composer Herman Rechberger 'prepared' ten of the instruments (by placing foreign objects on the bars) in his children's piece *Mobile 4* (1977).

✄ Gong

In orchestral parlance the 'tam-tam', this is a circular metal plate at least 80cm (32 inches) in diameter which is suspended from a frame and struck with a soft-headed stick. François-Joseph

A PORTABLE *GLOCKENSPIEL* MOUNTED UPON A LYRE-SHAPED STAND AND PLAYED BY A BANDSMAN OF THE **US ARMY AIR FORCE.**

Gossec, the Belgian composer, was the first to put it in the orchestra, in his *Funeral Music for Mirabeau* (1791).

✄ Marimba or Marimbaphone

A pitched invention of the early 20th century. Its shape resembles a xylophone but with resonating tubes hanging below the keys to give a soft sonority. The American composer Paul Creston wrote a concerto for it in 1940, and the Japanese composer Teruyaki Noda included one in his Quintet for three flutes and bass (1968).

Tambourine

A round, frame drum with metal discs inserted loosely in the frame. These jingle when the skin is hit or rubbed, or the whole instrument shaken. The earliest tambourines of prehistoric times differ little from the modern instrument, which entered the orchestra only in 1779, with Gluck's opera *Echo et Narcisse*. A craze for accompanying the piano with tambourine in dances and sonatas was short-lived around 1800, but modern composers use the instrument regularly. A long tambourine roll accompanies a cadenza in Shostakovich's Cello Concerto No. 2 (1966).

Triangle

A companion of cymbals and bass drum in European 'Turkish' music, the triangle is the orchestral instrument with the least mass but the most penetrating voice. A triangular rod of steel hit with a steel beater, it once bore metal rings to still further intensify the sound. Again, opera, ever watchful for telling effects, was responsible for bringing it into the orchestra, but what work

ROY AYERS PLAYS THE VIBRAPHONE, WHICH FOUND ITS PLACE IN JAZZ THROUGH MILT JACKSON.

John Cage
INVENTOR AND COMPOSER

One Tuesday in Seattle in 1938 John Cage was asked by the dancer Syvilla Fort to write a Baccanale for the following Friday. A percussion group was indicated, but none was available at such notice. Cage improvised by means of applying kitchen utensils (cutlery, crockery, metal dishes, for example) to the strings of a piano to modify its tone. Unfortunately, they slid about when the strings vibrated. Undeterred, he turned to woodscrews, erasers, mutes and bolts, fixing each type to a specified string at a precise distance from damper or bridge.

This experiment proved to be the first in a long line of works by Cage for 'prepared' piano. In addition he experimented with electronics, in one instance applying contact microphones to a glass of water containing dissolving aspirins). In 1952 he 'composed' the notorious 4' 33" in which, for that length of time, any instrumentalists present (and any may be) must not play.

CAGE ALSO WROTE A LARGE QUANTITY OF MUSIC FOR PERCUSSION ALONE:
- Quartet (1935)
- Trio (1936)
- *First Construction (in Metal)*, for six percussion (1939)
- *Second Construction*, for four percussion (1941)
- *Credo in Us*, for four percussion (1942)
- *Imaginary Landscape 2*, for five percussion (1942)
- *Imaginary Landscape 3*, for six percussion (1942)
- *The Wonderful Widow of 18 Springs*, for one voice and piano (1942), the piano to remain closed while its case is played
- *A Flower*, for voice and closed piano (1950)
- Music for *Carillon 1* (1952), for bells
- Music for *Carillon 23* (1954), for bells
- *7' 10.554"*, for percussion (1956)
- Music for *Carillon 4* (1966), for bells

it graced at the Hamburg Opera in 1710 is not known. It invariably accompanied cymbals in 'Turkish' music during the 18th century but assumed more independent roles in Paganini's Violin Concertos No. 2 (1821) and No. 4 (1830).

Tubular Bells

In an orchestral environment tubular bells are considerably more convenient than real bells, the main advantage being that of portability. Tuned lengths of narrow metal tubing are hung from a frame and struck with hard mallets at the top edge to create a convincing bell like tone. Their invention during the 1880s by a Coventry manufacturer, John Hampton, was quickly followed

by their first concert appearance: in Arthur Sullivan's *Golden Legend* (1886).

Vibraphone

Called vibraharp when it was invented in 1910, this instrument has been known by its current name since 1927. It is happier in a jazz setting than in the orchestra. Like the marimba, it resembles a xylophone with two ranges of tuned metal keys, and with vertical resonators underneath. Darius Milhaud appears to have been the first to use it 'seriously', in his incidental music for Claudel's play *L'annonce faite à Marie* (1932). The Japanese composer Akira Miyoshi has awarded the vibraphone a concerto (1969).

℘ *Whip*

A name which reflects this instrument's sound. Its alternative name, 'slapstick', betrays its construction. It is difficult to imagine a musical use for a whip in ancient times, unless a real whip was cracked as an audible guide should the rhythm flag. A third name for the instrument, 'jazz stick', suggests that it is a fairly recent phenomenon. In the early days of jazz, with bandleaders competing for the latest gimmick to surprise the crowds, whips were only one of the devices to see service, but more formal uses demanded a specially designed noise-maker. Modern orchestral whips consist of two pieces of wood hinged near the end and kept apart at an angle by a weak spring. When required, the woods are brought together with a sharp crack. Probably the best known example of the use of the whip occurs at the opening of Ravel's Piano Concerto in G (1931). It is also heard, punctually and in its place, in the galaxy of instruments paraded in Britten's *Young Person's Guide to the Orchestra* (1946).

℘ *Wind Machine*

This noise maker for special effects might be expected in the opera house, the usual spawning ground for such things, but it seems, as far as its

well known appearances are concerned, to be more welcome in the concert hall. As its name suggests, it creates artificial wind sounds by mechanical means. When Ralph Vaughan Williams used it in his *Sinfonia Antartica* (1952), written originally for the film *Scott of the Antarctic*, he requested that the wind machine

♭ A DRUM-TYPE WIND MACHINE. WHEN THE HANDLE IS TURNED A CONTINUOUS BUT VARIABLE SWISHING SOUND IS CREATED TO REPRESENT A HIGH WIND.

should be played out of sight of the audience, so that the chilling effect of the sound comes as a complete surprise. There are two models of wind machine. The less frequently encountered is an electric fan to the blades of which have been fitted slats of wood. More familiar is the rotating drum version, the drum covered by canvas or silk which rubs against wood laths or cardboard tongues when a handle is turned. The faster the rotation of either model, the higher the pitch. However, with such an instrument precise pitch is neither possible nor desirable.

❊ Woodblocks

A catch-all name for Chinese blocks, temple blocks and Korean temple blocks. Each type is different, their only point of similarity being that each is constructed from a round or rounded block of wood. The original Oriental blocks sometimes exceeded 60cm (24 inches) in diameter, their resonant tones being used in religious ceremonies. Orchestral blocks are about a maximum of 15cm (6 inches) in diameter and have a slit in the lower face. They are ranged before the player who hits them with a knobbed, wooden stick. An obvious use is in imitation of horses' or other quadrupeds' hooves, but in rapid action they have been used to imitate the chattering of apes. The first composer to use woodblocks was Sir William Walton, in *Façade* (1923). They also appear in two piano concertos: by George Gershwin (1925) and Constant Lambert (1931).

Confusion surrounds the terminology applied to these instruments. Sometimes the term 'woodblock' is used for a modern adaptation of the ancient design, made from a hollow piece of rectangular wood and played with side drum sticks. A further development of this type can sound two different notes. This has slits and wooden tongues on its upper surface and relates to the larger African message drum

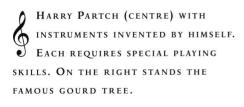

HARRY PARTCH (CENTRE) WITH INSTRUMENTS INVENTED BY HIMSELF. EACH REQUIRES SPECIAL PLAYING SKILLS. ON THE RIGHT STANDS THE FAMOUS GOURD TREE.

Richard Strauss used a species of wind machine in his tone-poem *Don Quixote* in 1897 (where, in the English translation of the score, it is described as a 'ventilator'), and – to add meteorological and atmospheric verisimilitude – in his highly descriptive 'Alpine' Symphony (1915).

❊ Xylophone

Slats of tuned wood ranged according to size and pitch are common in ethnic communities, a pointer to the concept's considerable antiquity. Hans Christian Lumbye was the first to score it, in his *Traumbilder* (1873); Saint-Saëns's *Danse Macabre*, a vivid portrayal of a dance of death in which the Devil plays the violin, followed a year later. István Lang wrote a concerto for xylophone (1961), and the Japanese composer Toshiro Mayuzumi composed a *concertino* for it in 1965.

THE *Partch* PHENOMENON ❊

In addition to inventing a number of stringed instruments and his own tuning system, the American experimentalist Harry Partch built many novel percussion instruments. He developed his own scale of 43 notes to the octave and composed music for the strange instruments he invented. Among the percussion were:

CONE GONGS Cone-shaped metal structures about one metre (3 feet) high and 35cm (14 inches) in diameter round the base, supported on a wooden structure;

GOURD TREE Literally a tree branch supported on a wooden stand and hung with gourds which are struck with sticks.

In addition, the following percussion were invented by Partch. Their names and materials give a hint as to their sound quality:

Bass marimba (wood)
Boo(bam) (bamboo)
Cloud chamber bowls (glass)
Diamond marimba (wood)
Marimba eroica (wood)
Mazda marimba (glass)
Quadrangularis roverscum, spoils of war (glass, wood, metal)
Zymo-xyl (glass, wood, metal)

❊ Xylorimba

This early 20th-century development of the xylophone has a much extended range. After its initial trial runs in music halls, Alban Berg included it in his *Three Pieces for Orchestra* (1915). In his Hymnody (1963) for chamber ensemble, the Spanish-born English composer Roberto Gerhard required that a xylorimba be played by two percussionists simultaneously.

Rare Percussion

Bells

The first composer to use bells in a 'serious' context apparently was Georg Melchior Hoffmann in a funeral cantata *Schlage doch* (c.1730), formerly attributed to J. S. Bach. The score calls for *campanelle*, which is translated as '2 Glöckchen' ('little bells'). The opera *Camille* (1791) by Nicolas-Marie Dalayrac requires the ringing of church bells, as does Ignaz Pleyel's *La Révolution du Dix Août* of the following year. Giacomo Meyerbeer's opera *Les Huguenots* (1836) demanded a specially made huge bell, and Tchaikovsky's *1812* Overture (1880) called for 'all the bells of Moscow'.

Bell Bars

These are literally bars of metal that ring like bells when struck. These are included by the dozen in David Bedford's children's piece *Whitefield Music 1* (1967), along with a dozen milk bottles and four drums. Marrowbones-and-cleaver, once regularly heard at butchers' weddings, can make a similar sound.

Bird Scare

Used in the Symphony No. 1, 'Gothic' (1927), by Havergal Brian. Percussionist James Blades identifies the bird scare as no more than a rattle, an alarm signal familiar in Spain and Latin America as the *matraca* and on football terraces as a noise maker.

Cannon

Tchaikovsky's well-known cannon shots in the *1812* Overture were presaged by those in François-Joseph Gossec's Overture in C, *Le Triomphe de la Republique ou le Corps de Grand Pré*, published in Paris in 1793.

NAUTICAL TUBULAR BELLS – CAPTAIN LINDELL OF SS *STRATHMORE* PHOTOGRAPHED IN 1935; SEE PAGE 25.

Chains

Large and small, dragged along the floor and shaken, are requested, respectively, in Arnold Schoenberg's *Gurrelieder* (1901) and Havergal Brian's 'Gothic' Symphony (see Bird scare entry, above).

Cuckoo Clock

Together with an alarm clock bell, this appears in Leroy Anderson's *The Syncopated Clock* (1945). The sound of a cuckoo, played by a toy, flute or recorder, is heard in the 'Toy Symphony' attributed to Joseph Haydn but actually part of a Cassation in G (1756) by Mozart's father, Leopold. Therein are also heard quail, nightingale, toy trumpet and rattle.

Drum Sticks

These play a vital part in the percussion section of course, but they usually have a drum to hit. It is reported that Isaac Albéniz, the Spanish composer, dispensed with the latter accoutrement and instructed that in one of his works the percussionist is to beat the music desk with drum sticks. This recalls Rossini's eccentric instruction to his second violins in the overture to the comic opera *Il Signor Bruschino* (1813) to strike their music stands (or, according to one report, their candle holders) with the wood of their bows.

℅ Dulcitone

A keyboard instrument in which hammers strike a row of tuning forks within the cabinet. The result is not strong in tone, the dulcitone being essentially for domestic enjoyment, but Vincent d'Indy imaginatively suggested its use in his *Song of the Bells* (1883). In most performances, where the bell-like instrument's tone is expected to fill the recital room, the part is taken instead by *glockenspiel*, see page 24.

℅ Sandpaper

As unlikely a musical instrument as one will ever meet, perhaps, but Leroy Anderson in his *Sandpaper Ballet* (1954) required sheets to be rubbed on a hard surface as a rhythmic accompaniment. The effect is not unlike the 'soft-shoe shuffle' once in vogue in music halls.

℅ Saw

Also optimistically called musical saw, this was another favourite music-hall gimmick. The saw was played with a violin bow to create a ghostly wailing sound, to the amazement of the audience. Several composers have scored for it, notably the Japanese Toshiro Mayuzumi in *Tone Pleromas 55* (1955), where it is joined by five saxophones, and in *Mikrokosmos* (1957), where its colleagues are claviolin (an electronic keyboard instrument), guitar, vibraphone, piano and percussion. Darius Milhaud put the saw to more percussive use when he called for it to be hit with a drumstick in his *Cinq Etudes*, Op. 63 (1920), only one of the outrageous effects in a score for piano and orchestra that took polytonality to new extremes with four independent fugues playing simultaneously in different keys. This caused a near-riot at its Paris premiere the following year.

℅ Spoons

Ordinary household ones are rattled together in George Auric's ballet *Les Matelots* (1924). We may again thank music hall, and perhaps also the street musician, for familiarizing us with the rhythmic possibilities inherent in spoons.

℅ Thunder Sheet

A noise-maker par excellence, this is an orchestral instrument borrowed from the theatrical effects department, where several means were employed to imitate meteorological roaring. In some, heavy metal balls were dropped onto leather, in others they were rotated in a barrel or rolled down a wooden ramp. The orchestral version is only slightly less inconvenient: a suspended metal sheet, 3.65m (10 feet) high and 1.2m (4 feet) wide, is attacked with soft headed sticks, its resonance being increased if necessary by its being placed against a bass drum. Today, old fashioned is the organization that fails to use the convenience of pre-recorded real thunder. Richard Strauss, in the days before tape recorders (1915), used a thunder sheet to depict stormy weather in his 'Alpine' Symphony, but John Cage was somewhat more demanding in his *First Construction* (1942): he wanted five thunder sheets of different sizes.

℅ Tumba

A long (1m/3 feet), thin drum, usually found in pairs and played by the hands, the pitch varying

𝄞 A KEYBOARD-OPERATED *CARILLON*. THE KEY AND PEDAL MOVEMENTS ARE CONVEYED BY METAL RODS TO CLAPPERS WHICH STRIKE THE BELLS HIGH ABOVE IN THE 'BELL CHAMBER'.

according to the area of the head being hit. Kurt Wege's arrangements of Leroy Anderson's *Jazz Pizzicato* (1949) and *Fiddle-Faddle* (1952) included them and they are common (as conga drums) in Latin American dance bands. To Pakistanis the word *tumba* refers to a long lute.

℅ Typewriter

Perhaps a threatened species in these days of word processors, but still recognizable by its quiet clicking in some offices. When Erik Satie in *Parade* (1917), Ferde Grofé in *Tabloid* (1947), Leroy Anderson in *The Typewriter* (1950) and Rolf Liebermann in *Concert des changes* (before 1964) required typewriters, the machine made a much more piercing sound, such that in Liebermann's work it could be heard equally with the cash registers and calculating machines which are its co-soloists in the score. 𝄡

Electronic Instruments

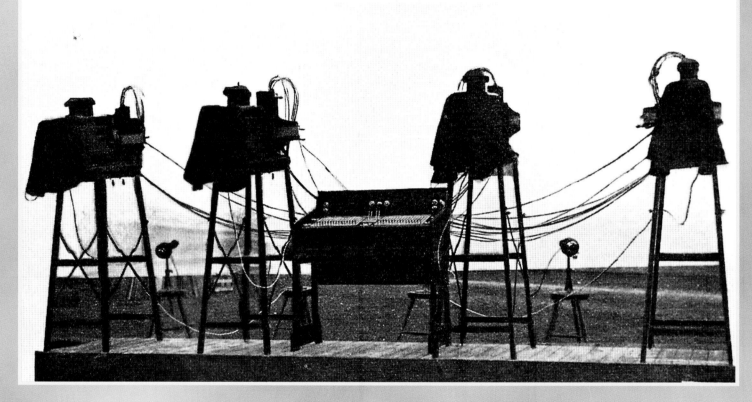

The invention and development of electronically generated music has depended on several disparate factors: a number of scientific inventions, on acoustical research into how sounds are generated and their fundamental characteristics and on the strong desire of some pioneering composers to explore sounds not made by conventional instruments. The first attempt to power musical instruments with electricity was made in 1762 by the Bohemian, Prokop Divis. His *Denis d'or* was described as an 'orchestrion' because it could imitate most string and wind sounds. It was keyboard-operated. There were similar experiments throughout the 18th and 19th centuries. The development of greatest significance in the evolution of electronic instruments was Alexander Graham Bell's invention of the telephone in 1876. This demonstrated that sound could be converted to electric signals and vice versa. Emile Berliner, in 1877, developed a telephone receiver and, ten years later, a disc recording machine he called 'gramophone'. The latter helped to amend the weaknesses in Thomas Edison's 'talking machine' of 1877, a 'phonograph' for recording and reproducing sound. In 1898 a Danish scientist, Valdemar Poulsen, invented the 'telegraphone', the first magnetic recording machine. Its use of piano wire on which to record proved problematical; a satisfactory result was achieved only when magnetic tape was introduced in 1935. This remained the basis of recording until the present, when digital recording onto hard disc looks set to replace it.

Electronics vs. Music

These inventions, made at a time of exciting discoveries in every scientific and mechanical field, were not obviously connected with music. Indeed, orchestral and operatic music might seem to be the antithesis of electronic music. Yet, from the second half of the 19th century, composers such as Wagner, Richard Strauss, Mahler, Debussy, Scriabin and Schoenberg were all searching for new sonorities. Theodore Boehm and Adolphe Sax had made woodwind and brass instruments more chromatically flexible, louder and more reliable. Soon, the search for different sonorities that led Wagner to use a new tuba, and Strauss to write for the heckelphone, would encourage others to explore the possibilities of musical sounds produced by means other than existing instruments.

The Search for New Music

As important as the development of new instruments and electrical machines was the exploration of sound itself. In 1863 Hermann von Helmholtz published his seminal study on this subject, *Die Lehre von den Tonempfindungen als physiologische Grundlage für die Theorie der Musik* (translated by A. J. Ellis in 1875 as *On the Sensations of Tone as a Physiological Basis for the Theory of Music*). Helmholtz demonstrated

that the sound produced by any instrument can be divided into several parts. Most important for the timbre, or nature, of the sound is the 'formant', a term for how a sound is characterized by the shape, dimension and material of an instrument. Also important for the timbre is the 'onset', 'attack' or first impact of a note, for this contains its character. After the 'onset', notes of all instruments are remarkably similar, as can now be demonstrated on tape by removing the 'onset' and playing the remaining sound. It is the combination of overtones (vibrations additional to the basic note) that give the 'onset' its identity. Thus, Helmholtz not only isolated the elements that constitute the timbre of a note, but postulated the possibility of creating a note without overtones – in effect, a 'pure' note. For this, an electric machine was needed.

Dispassionate scientific investigation and a passionate desire to write music for the new industrial age of the early 20th century were in equal measure responsible for bringing all these elements together to produce the first experiments with electrically generated sound.

LEFT: LASZLO'S *FARBLICHTKLAVIER*.
BELOW: POULSEN'S 'TELEGRAPHONE'.

First Generation

One of the earliest instruments to put Helmholtz's discoveries into practice was 'Sounding Staves', patented in 1896 by the American, Dr. Thaddeus Cahill. Designed to be a synthetic orchestra of 'pure' sounds operated by a single player, it could regulate the number of upper harmonics contained in a pitch, thus achieving a new timbral control of notes. Its chief novelties were the range of sounds it could achieve and its capacity to change sounds derived from traditional instruments. Cahill's machine was called variously a *Dynamophone* or a *Telharmonium*, with Cahill preferring the latter. The aim of this invention, according to Cahill, was 'to generate music electrically with tones of good quality and great power and with perfect musical expression, and to distribute music electrically generated by what we may term "original electrical generation" from a central point to translating instruments located at different points'. The prototype was built in 1900 in Washington, but the first full-sized version was not completed until 1906 in New York. Unfortunately for Cahill, his invention was ahead of its time and his instruments were eventually sold as scrap, although many later developments were based on them.

In 1906 another American, Lee De Forest, invented a vacuum tube (also called a thermionic valve or triode tube) which could control electrical current precisely and could be used to generate, amplify, modulate and detect electrical current. It greatly improved the amplification of sound on the gramophone and radio, as well as generating audio signals in tube oscillators. This was but the beginnings of what De Forest eventually perfected in 1915 as the oscillator, which still forms the basis of electronically generated sound. The oscillator made it possible to generate accurately pitched sounds from electrical signals and paved the way for the invention of further electronic musical instruments.

INSTRUMENTS OF FUTURISM

THE MOST SYSTEMATIC experimentation with new instruments and novel sounds in the years either side of the First World War occurred in Italy, under the influence of Futurism. The credo of Futurism was made known to the world in 1909 by the Italian poet Filippo Marinetti, in his *Foundation and Manifesto of Futurism*, in which he celebrated the energy of contemporary industrial life and its machines. The search for a new kind of music was soon underway. In 1911 the musician Francesco Pratella published *The Technical Manifesto of Futurist Music*, in which he argued for the use of microtones and sounds to replace

music by "venal flatterers of the public's base taste", by which he primarily meant Puccini and his very successful verismo operas.

Ironically, it was not the composer Pratella but the painter Luigi Russolo who had the most impact on Futurism's musical thinking and thereby on the development of electronic musical instruments. In 1916 he enshrined his ideas in another Futurist manifesto, *L'arte de rumori*, in which he criticized traditional theories of harmony and advocated a new music that would use different sounds, collected from everyday life (the musical equivalent of *objet trouvé*). Russolo

THE FUTURISTS IN 1912: (LEFT TO RIGHT) RUSSOLO, CARLO CARRE, MARINETTI, UMBERTO BOCCIONI AND GINO SEVERINI.

had been pursuing these ideals since 1913, in which year he produced, together with Ugo Piatti, the first of his *Intonarumori*.

Each of the *Intonarumori* consisted of a brightly coloured box from which at the front projected a horn, like an early gramophone, and at the back a handle which the player turned to produce the noise. Inside the box of most of the

Russolo's Inventions

%

INTONARUMORI

A group of machines/instruments designed by Russolo and Ugo Piatti in Milan between 1913 and 1921 to produce various noises. (The word intonarumori means 'noise intoners'.) Russolo divided the groups of noises into six categories:

Rumbles	Whistles	Whispers	Screeches	NOISES OBTAINED	VOICES OF ANIMALS
Roars	Hisses	Murmurs	Creaks	BY PERCUSSION	AND MEN
Explosions	Snorts	Mumbles	Rustles	ON:	Shouts
Crashes		Grumbles	Buzzes	metal	Screams
Splashes		Gurgles	Crackles	wood	Groans
Booms			Scrapes	skin	Shrieks
				stone	Howls
				terracotta	Laughs
					Wheezes
					Sobs

ARCO ENARMONICO

A special bow for stringed instruments devised by Russolo in Milan in 1925. It was made of a rod wound round with wire so that it had a slightly ridged surface. The stringed instrument was bowed in the normal way, but the sound it produced was different: coarse *legato* and rapid repetitions could be achieved. The sounds resembled the rumbles and whispers of Russolo's *Intonarumori*. A reconstruction of the bow was made in Venice in 1977.

PIANO ENARMONICO

A keyboard instrument developed by Russolo in the Thirties in which each piano key makes a moving driving-belt come into contact with a long coiled spring mounted on a resonance box. The principle on which it operates is similar to that of a hurdy-gurdy

Intonarumori was a wheel, made either of wood or metal, which rotated against a gut or metal string. The tension of the string could be altered by a lever to give different pitches, including microtones. At one end of the string and attached to the horn was a stretched skin (like that of a drum), whose vibration, along with the string, made the required noise. Various modifications were made to this design, depending on the noise desired.

Russolo's vocabulary of new sounds included noises from objects and machines, and also from nature and humans. In 1914 he devised a graphic form of notating these, entitled *Enharmonic Notation for the Futurist Intonarumori*, in which a horizontal line denotes the duration of a sound. This notation was later adopted by Cage and Stockhausen.

Russolo's first concerts on his noise machines took place in Milan in 1913 and caused an uproar. Subsequent performances were held in Genoa and London, but it was in 1920s Paris, the pre-eminent centre for experimentation, that these machines aroused the most sympathetic interest, attracting the attention of Stravinsky, Ravel, Milhaud and, most significantly, Edgard Varèse.

Russolo and Marinetti, though not Pratella, remained faithful to Futurist ideals. As late as 1933, when the white-heat of the early polemics had cooled and the political situation in Italy was increasingly unfavourable to experimental art, Russolo and Marinetti were working with a Futurist Radiophonic Theatre in which tiny sounds, inaudible to the human ear, could be amplified and used in musical compositions.

EDGAR VARESE WAS ONE OF THE FIRST MAJOR COMPOSERS TO ENTHUSIASTICALLY EMBRACE THE POSSIBILITIES OF ELECTRONIC MUSIC.

IMPORTANT
Electronic Instruments

✄

THEREMIN In 1920 the Russian scientist Lev Theremin invented a *thérémin* (as it is best known in its French form), consisting of an oscillator controlled by movement of the hands. The closer the operating hand approaches the antenna (which sticks vertically out of the instrument) the higher the pitch climbs, while the other hand controls the volume by its proximity to a metal loop. The *thérémin* gained some fame through the performances of a few virtuosi who could demonstrate its highly expressive, almost vocal, qualities, but never became widely used because of the great difficulty of playing it. Some attempts are being made to revive interest in it. Perhaps its most famous orchestral use was in Varèse's *Ecuatorial*, which originally called for two *thérémins*. At the work's premiere in 1934, the volume of the two *thérémins* proved so difficult to control that Varèse replaced them with two *ondes martenots* (see below). In 1926 Theremin invented an electric harmonium capable of dividing the octave into 1200 pitches, a refinement far too subtle for the human ear to detect.

ONDES MARTENOT Probably the most successful post-Cahill electronic musical instrument, the *ondes martenot* was patented in 1922 by the Frenchman Maurice Martenot and produced by him in 1928. It has oscillating valves similar to those of the *thérémin*, but pitch can be controlled more easily: players move their fingers along a wire stretched in front of a five-octave keyboard. Timbral and tonal changes are effected by means of buttons and keys. Like the *thérémin*, the *ondes martenot* is capable of a moving, disembodied vocal-like timbre and of achieving great volume, audible above even a large orchestra. Messiaen used it particularly effectively in his *Trois Petites Liturgies de la Présence Divine* (1944) and *Turgangalîla* Symphony (1946–8). Other composers to have used the instrument include Honegger, Jolivet and Boulez.

ABOVE: *ONDES MARTENOT* PLAYED BY GINETTE MARTENOT, THE SISTER OF THE INSTRUMENT'S INVENTOR.

HAMMOND ORGAN Invented in 1935 by the American Laurens Hammond, who also invented the *solovox*, chord organ and *novachord*, this was intended to replace the pipe organ for pseudo-ecclesiastical and domestic uses. The Hammond organ resembled it in having two manuals and a pedal board, but the sound was produced by electrical means similar to the *ondes martenot*. In the 1960s Stockhausen became interested in its potential and released it from its intended original purpose, notably in *Mikrophonie II* (1965). It has also been widely used in jazz and pop music.

TRAUTONIUM This instrument, invented by the German Friedrich Trautwein in 1930, proved popular at the time with some German composers, not least because of its ability to obtain varieties of tone-colour and, with relative ease, accurate pitches. Richard Strauss and Hindemith both experimented with it.

COMPOSERS OF ELECTRONIC MUSIC USED FILTER MACHINES TO CREATE THEIR COMPOSITIONS.

MUSIQUE CONCRETE

IT IS ONE of the strange ironies of the evolution of electronic music and instruments that the founder of *musique concrète*, Pierre Schaeffer, did not know of Russolo's experiments with noise machines. Initially, Schaeffer used 78 rpm records and relatively unsophisticated mechanical means to produce his new music. From the 1950s onwards he used the magnetic tape recorder which, although invented in 1935, was not widely available until after the Second World War. This proved an indispensable part of the new developments, because it could store and retrieve sounds and compositions, and because eventually it could be used to alter sounds.

Schaeffer was a radio technician by training, not a musician. In 1948, while working for French Radio, he developed a means of using several tape recorders to extract sounds from pre-existing recordings. What he could do with the sounds was relatively limited: the techniques available enabled him only to exclude some parts of the sounds, play them backwards ('tape reversal') or combine different sounds ('collage'). Even so, he managed to achieve a wider range of sounds than Russolo, employing means that were simpler to use but much more sophisticated in their results.

The distinctive feature of *musique concrète* is that the original sounds, from which the final compositions were made, were pre-existing and non-electronically generated. The term 'concrète' was used to denote both that the sounds from which the pieces were derived were from concrete (ie, 'tangible') natural sources, and that the pieces were composed 'concretely' onto the tapes rather than abstractly in the head of the composer using notation as a guide to subsequent performance.

Schaeffer, like Russolo, utilized sounds from everyday life, and began making compositions with objects such as clashing saucepan lids. From the outset, though, *musique concrète* also encompassed pre-existing musical sounds as sources. Schaeffer was also attracted to the multiple sounds obtainable from the piano other than by playing the keyboard. On 5 October 1948 he broadcast a 'concert of noises' in which five works were 'played'. These included two 'études' derived from piano sounds (for whom the pianist was Boulez), and *Etude aux casseroles*, which used sounds taken from, among other sources, spin-

MUSIQUE CONCRETE MARKED A TURNING AWAY FROM ELECTRICAL MEANS OF COMPOSITION (HERE A TRAUTONIUM).

ning saucepan lids, boats and human voices.

In 1949 Schaeffer was joined by Pierre Henry. Two years later French Radio rewarded the efforts of the two men by constructing a special studio which included tape recorders, sound filters and many other means for creating and manipulating sounds. In the pioneering work completed here, Schaeffer and Henry were considerably aided by their technical assistant, Jacques Poullin.

MAJOR COMPOSERS OF

Musique Concrète

※

PIERRE SCHAEFFER was the founder of *musique concrète* at the station of French Radio. His *Etude aux chemins de fer* (Study for Railroad Trains) (1948) was the first 'concrete' composition. He composed less frequently after the early 1950s and spent more time training and advising other composers in his studio.

PIERRE HENRY was one of the most prolific composers of *musique concrète*. He worked at the studio of French Radio until 1958 after which he set up his own studio, Studio Apsome, with the choreographer Maurice Béjart. His *Symphonie pour homme seul* (1949–50) (written jointly with Schaeffer) was based principally on 'human' noises, such as breathing, whistling, talking and laughing, together with some transformed orchestral sounds and effects such as 'footsteps'. The piece was so evocative that it was later used as a ballet. In 1955 Henry and Schaeffer worked on the first *musique-concrète* opera, *Orphée 53*. Two other works by Henry are among the best-known *musique-concrète* works: *Le voyage* (1961–62) and *Variations pour une porte et un soupir* (Variations for a door and a sigh) (1963).

LUCIANO BERIO was one of the many young composers to work with Schaeffer in Paris. Among his most celebrated *musique-concrète* pieces was *Thema* (1958), subtitled *Omaggio à Joyce*. The sound source was his then-wife, the singer Cathy Berberian, reading part of Molly's soliloquy from James Joyce's *Ulysses*. After almost two minutes the voice is dissolved into a series of onomatopoeic fragmentations of the text. The 'oo' in a word such as 'blooming' is enormously extended to suggest its meaning, as is the 'ss' in 'hiss'. The result is an evocative and suggestive interpretation of the original text, achieved solely by manipulating the sound of the original reading.

STEVE REICH (shown below in rehearsal) Many of Reich's minimalist compositions owe much to electronic effects, particularly tape loops. The idea for his *concrète* piece *Come Out* (1966) came from the events associated with a riot in Harlem in 1964 in which a young African-American, Daniel Hamm, was arrested for murder. Hamm was beaten by the police and in order to gain hospitalization had to "… open the bruise up and let the bruise blood come out to show them". Reich repeats this phrase three times before selecting the last five words for continuous repetition on tape loops of different lengths, each repetition getting the voice further and further 'out of phase' with itself until it became unrecognizable. The work was recorded on two channels so needs two speakers for performance.

Paris was not the only city to set up a studio dedicated to electronic music. In New York, Vladimir Ussachevsky and Otto Luening founded a studio at Columbia University in 1951. Among the first compositions to come out of this studio were *Transposition and Reverberation* (1952), a collaborative effort, and Ussachevsky's *Sonic Contours* (1952). Both works used piano sounds as their basis, showing that, unlike the French, the Americans preferred using pre-existing 'musical' sounds rather than 'natural', 'everyday' sounds.

Musique concrète had to be painstakingly assembled by splicing together many bits of tape, so much of the music seemed to be full of rather angular and sudden changes of sound and dynamics. In time, however, greater sophistication led to improvements in the ability to transform sounds and to achieve a wider range of different effects. French *musique concrète* is often suggestively sombre and dark, reflecting a French aesthetic more than an inevitable electronic aesthetic. Later American composers discovered lighter textures and even humour. The growth in sounds and suggestive effects, as well as the fact that most of the early studios were connected with radio stations, inevitably led to these early *concrète* experiments finding their way into radio effects and, eventually, films.

Musique concrète was at first used to define music whose sound sources were natural. The new technology (and some of the old) could also generate its own sounds, and quite rapidly composers such as Stockhausen and Xenakis started using a mixture of electronically generated sounds as well as natural and musical noises. At first, electronically generated music and *musique concrète* appeared as opposites, but over the years they have merged and composers happily use either or both sources. The heyday of purely *musique concrète* lasted from the late 1940s until the end of the 1950s. During this time the French studio attracted many leading composers, from young neophytes such as Boulez, Stockhausen and Messiaen, to established figures like Milhaud.

❧ *Experimentation: Cologne*

Slightly later than Schaeffer's experiments in Paris, Herbert Eimert founded a studio in Cologne (at Westdeutscher Rundfunk) dedicated to experimenting with electronically generated rather than 'natural' or 'instrumental' sounds. He was soon joined by Stockhausen and together they embarked on the creation of what they termed 'Elektronische Musik'. Their starting point was an instrument called the 'melochord', devised by Werner Meyer-Eppler and Robert Beyer in Cologne in 1950. This produced sounds by means of oscillators and other purely electronic means. What particularly attracted Stockhausen was the complete control he would have over sounds. Musical experiments since the late 1940s had been trying to extend the serialization of twelve tones (begun by Schoenberg in the 1920s and subsequently by Webern) to include rhythms, durations and so on, as Messiaen had done in his pioneering *Modes de valeurs et d'intensités* (1949). In performance much of the precision that had been intended by the composer was lost in the license that a performer was obliged or felt able to take. The prospect of the composer being able to control a piece from its inception to its final production was particularly alluring.

Stockhausen's first attempts – his two *Studien* – showed the way, but his most outstanding early work, the magnificent *Gesang der Jünglinge* (1955–6), represents the kind of compromise between *concrète* and purely electronic sounds that would become increasingly evident in the works of many other composers. In the *Gesang* a boy's voice singing the Benedicite is processed and mixed with electronic sounds. Originally 'performances' of this work were to be played on

𝄞 BY THE MID 1950S STOCKHAUSEN WAS THE ACKNOWLEDGED LEADER OF THE AVANT-GARDE.

FIVE PIONEERS OF
Electronic composition
❧

EDGARD VARESE was an influential avant-garde composer. He used two *thérémins* in his *Ecuatorial* and wrote two mainly electronic pieces: *Good Friday Procession in Verges* (1955–6) and *Poème Electronique* (1957–8).

KARLHEINZ STOCKHAUSEN has been one of the pioneers of using purely electronic, as well as *concrète,* sounds. His *Gesang der Jünglinge* set a new standard for electronic music, as did his later *Kontakte.* He pioneered using electronically prepared tapes in live performances.

JOHN CAGE was one of the most innovative experimenters with a wide range of computer-generated sounds. Following his experiments with non-music *concrète* sounds, in 1951 he wrote *Imaginary landscape 4* for 12 radios and 24 operators. He pioneered, with the pianist David Tudor, live electronic music with his *Music for Amplified Toy Pianos,* and *Cartridge Music* (both 1960).

IANNIS XENAKIS assisted le Corbusier in the design of the Philips exhibit in Brussels in 1958 at which Varèse's *Poème Electronique* was performed. Fascinated by computers, he has devised a special kind of music based on the notion that, depending on chance, music will eventually conclude itself, using computers to help calculate this. Among his most ambitious pieces is *Hibiki-Hana-Ma* (1970), written for 12 tapes sounding from 800 speakers.

MILTON BABBITT is one of the most important American composers to have used electronic means for composing. Included among his major works are *Composition for Synthesizer* (1970), *Philomel* (1964) for soprano, recorded soprano and synthesizer, and *Phenomena* (1974) for soprano and tape.

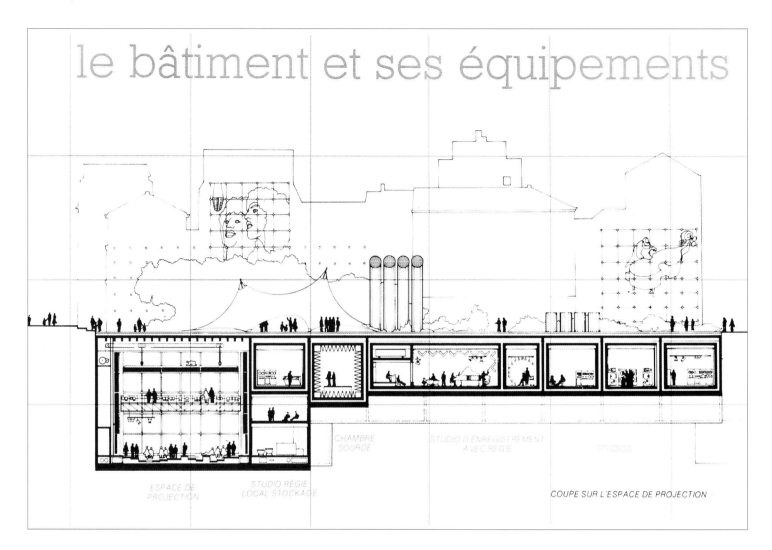

le bâtiment et ses équipements

CHAMBRE SOURDE · STUDIO D'ENREGISTREMENT AVEC RÉGIE · STUDIOS

ESPACE DE PROJECTION · STUDIO RÉGIE LOCAL STOCKAGE · COUPE SUR L'ESPACE DE PROJECTION

𝄞 A PLAN OF IRCAM, THE PARIS STUDIO DEDICATED TO THE DEVELOPMENT OF ELECTRONIC/COMPUTER MUSIC.

five speakers spaced around a concert hall, but this number was eventually reduced to four. At the same time, electronic devices began to be imitated by Stockhausen in purely instrumental works, such as *Klavierstück IX*, whose opening repeated chords and subsequent fragmentation mimic first reverberation and later the interplay of upper harmonics.

One of the great difficulties of early electronic music was that the composition of works took an inordinately long time, because the machines were not originally intended for the composition of music. Stockhausen's *Gesang der Jünglinge* took a year and a half to prepare. His

next major electronic piece, *Kontakte*, took two years. It was the synthesizer that eventually took the painstaking construction out of electronic composition and opened the way for both more flexible studio compositions and live 'real-time' interaction between computers and live musicians and their instruments.

✶ *Experimentation: Brussels And New York*

Meanwhile, composers elsewhere continued to experiment with the technology at their disposal. One of the most astonishing pieces of early electronic composition was the *Poème Electronique*, written by the 70-year-old Edgard Varèse for the Philips Pavilion at the 1958 Brussels World Fair.

The pavilion was designed by the Greek architect and composer Iannis Xenakis and the French architect Le Corbusier. Varèse's music, projected from 350 loudspeakers, was accompanied by lighting effects and slide projections. The sounds, a mixture of *concrète* and electronically produced, were recorded on three-channel tape with two of the channels being reserved for reverberation and stereo effects.

The wide divide between the conflicting aims of Paris and Cologne in the 1950s led some composers to work elsewhere, though at first their choice was limited due to the scarcity of electronic studios. This situation began to change in the late 1950s with studios in New York, at Columbia University (1951), the Electronic Studio in Tokyo at Japanese Radio (1953), the Studio de Musique Electronique in Brussels

(1958), and, perhaps as significant as any, the Studio di Fonologia at Italian Radio in Milan (1958). Not only did Italian composers such as Maderna and Berio work in Milan, but so did one of the most imaginative and innovative composers to experiment with electronic music, John Cage.

Cage had already experimented with electronically processed sounds, in his series of *Imaginary Landscapes* (1:1939, 2:1942, 3:1942). In the first he had used early experimental test records of pure sound played on variable speed turntables; and in the second he had added to the five percussionists an amplified coil of wire. In the third the six percussionists are also required to operate an audio frequency oscillator, an electric buzzer, recordings of different frequencies and an electronically amplified marimbula. The arrival of the tape recorder and more modern technology prompted Cage to compose *Williams Mix* and *Imaginary Landscape 5* (New York, 1952), and *Fontana Mix* (Milan 1958). Each of these pieces is a collage of different sounds. *Fontana Mix* moves away from the determinacy of the Cologne and Paris schools by giving minimal directions to the performer and allowing the prepared tape to be played with or without other accompanying music.

JOHN CAGE. HIS ACCEPTANCE OF THE ROLE OF CHANCE IN MUSIC BROADENED COMPOSITIONAL HORIZONS.

FOUR FAMOUS
Electronic Studios

COLUMBIA-PRINCETON ELECTRONIC MUSIC CENTER established in New York in 1951 by Ussachevsky and Luening. The Mark II RCA Music Synthesizer constructed by Belar and Olsen was transferred to the Center. This was the most advanced machine of its time and for a while gave the Center's resident composers an advantage in working with purely electronically generated sounds.

STUDIO FÜR ELEKTRONISCHE MUSIK, COLOGNE Established 1951 by Eimert. The first studio designed to produce music entirely by electronic means, it possessed the familiar devices of the *concrète* studio (variable speed tape recorders, filter, reverberating devices for creating echo effects, amplifiers, etc.) as well as oscillators and noise generators. Among the first works composed at the studio were Stockhausen's *Study I* (1953) and *Study II* (1954), as well as the pioneering synthesis of *concrète* and electronic, *Gesang der Jünglinge* (1956).

STUDIO DI FONOLOGIA, MILAN Established in 1953, this was one of the most productive early studios. From the beginning both *concrète* and electronic compositions were encouraged. Berio's *Thema: Omaggio à Joyce* (1958) is an example of the former, and Pousseur's *Scambi* (1957), which used only 'white noise' as its source, an example of the latter. Nono and Maderna also worked at the studio. Cage wrote his *Fontana Mix* there.

INSTITUT DE RECHERCHE ET DE COORDINATION ACOUSTIC/MUSIQUE (IRCAM) Established in Paris in 1976, since when it has aimed to be the most sophisticated and extensive studio for the production of electronic music in the world. Under the general direction of Boulez and paid for by the French government, it was designed for creating music and for research into acoustics and the psychology of how sounds are perceived. Emphasis is also placed on using the equipment as active participants in live music, especially transforming 'live sounds'. The studio is thus as much dedicated to *musique concrète* as to electronically generated music, though the distinction between these has become blurred if not extinct since the arrival of digital technology. In addition to Boulez, who used the IRCAM facilities for his work *Répons*, a wide range of composers have been invited to use the studio, from Berio, Trevor Wishart, Harrison Birtwistle, Jonathan Harvey and George Benjamin to the jazz composer George Lewis.

𝄞 SYNTHESIZERS

THE EARLIEST ELECTRONIC instruments, such as Russolo's *Intonarumori*, were unwieldy and capable of producing relatively few sounds. In the late 1950s and early 1960s composers and technicians were increasingly looking at ways of producing machines that were relatively simple to operate and offering a wider range of sounds. What composers wanted, and what eventually emerged in the shape of the synthesizer, was a single, easily operated machine capable of integrating the various means by which electronic sounds could be processed and generated.

The arrival of the synthesizer revolutionized electronic music making. It was both considerably cheaper than the elaborate machines produced hitherto and a time saver. Previously, each sound had had to be recorded onto tape, then each piece of tape cut to exactly the right length to give the sound its required duration. The synthesizer changed this.

℅ How the Synthesizer Works

Every synthesizer possesses a number of components, each of which has a specific function. The synthesizer's principal functions are to generate sounds and to process these sounds to suit the composer. Some of the components that fulfil these two requirements can be linked in a process known as 'patching'.

A synthesizer makes sounds, called audio signals, by means of an oscillator. This was specifically designed to produce pitches, called sine waves, that have no overtones. Normally, a note will travel through the ether like a wave. The notes generated by a synthesizer's sine wave produce a simple curve without 'overtones' or 'harmonics'. The pitch of a note can be altered by means of 'control voltages', which affect the power supply and thus move the pitch up or down. The sound-generating part of the synthesizer can produce a wide range of harmonics and create the sound known as 'white noise'.

There are many ways of processing the sounds on a synthesizer. The most basic one is to make the sound audible, which is done by an amplifier and through several monitoring speakers. Sometimes composers want to create the effect of a sound moving through space, in which case a 'spatial locator' is used to stagger the sound so that it reaches each speaker in turn rather than simultaneously. Sounds can also be combined to make a complex, or filtered so that some elements are removed or altered; a 'ring modulator' will achieve the former, a filter the latter. An artificial echo effect can be created by means of a 'reverberator'. 'Envelope generators' enable control of the attack and lengthen or shorten the decay of a sound.

The most significant control on a synthesizer is the keyboard (or keyboards), which looks like an ordinary piano keyboard but rarely behaves in the same way. The pitch of the keyboard can be altered, so that although each note is separated from its neighbour by a semitone, its pitch may not correspond to its equivalent key on a piano keyboard. The keyboard also controls the length of a note as well as its pitch. In some examples the keyboard is touch-sensitive so that several functions can be performed by the same key, depending on the way it is depressed or released.

THE YAMAHA VL7, ONE OF THE NEW GENERATION OF PORTABLE SYNTHESIZERS FOR COMMERCIAL USE.

✄ Types of Synthesizer

The first synthesizer was the RCA Mark II, developed at the Sarnoff Research Centre in New Jersey in 1955 and later housed at the Columbia-Princeton Electronic Studio (see page 39). Compared with what had gone before, it was much reduced in size due to the replacement of valves by transistors, although still quite bulky by later standards. The Mark II gave composers a marvellous new range of timbres and greatly increased their control over the sounds. This was of particular interest to those composers, such as Milton Babbitt, who wanted to extend the serialization of their music to include all elements, not just pitches or rhythms. The new synthesizer allowed the composer unprecedented control

JEAN-MICHEL JARRE, ONE OF THE FIRST COMPOSERS OF 'POPULAR' ELECTRONIC MUSIC.

and eliminated the distorting effect a live performance could have.

The RCA Mark II was superseded by smaller, more versatile machines. The two most important designers of the first commercially available synthesizers, which appeared in the mid-1960s, were Robert Moog and Donald Buchla. Moog's invention of a voltage-control amplifier meant that sounds could be controlled by voltages, relieving the composer of the chore of having to 'tune' each of his notes by hand before obtaining the right pitch or volume. The synthesizer performed the task automatically, and more quickly and accurately.

✄ Portables

The attempt to combine live performance with a pre-prepared tape is not new. Varèse, for instance, in his *Déserts* (1954), alternated passages for chamber ensemble with purely electronic sounds. Typically, Varèse contrasted

the timbres of the live instruments with the electronic ones. Later composers tried to combine and fuse the two sounds. Berio, for instance, in his *Différences* (1959), combined a live chamber group and recordings of the same instruments electronically processed.

However, the introduction of portable synthesizers has enabled electronics to take an active part in live performance, to generate sounds and combine them with those of other instruments. Paolo Ketoff designed and produced his Synket in Rome in 1964. Smaller and more portable than the Moog synthesizer, it was limited in having only three wave-selecting generators and one 'white noise' generator. The Synket also had limited 'patching' facilities – though for the most part the machine was hard-wired (ie, the wiring was predetermined and fixed in the machine and several outputs could not be combined) and three touch-sensitive two-octave keyboards. The first composer to use a Synket was the American John Eaton, in 1965, almost simultaneously with the first live performances using a Moog synthesizer.

RCA ELECTRONIC MUSIC SYNTHESIZER MARK I (1951–2): Mark II (1958) Compared with Moog's inventions these two RCA machines would not be categorized as synthesizers today but rather as programmable electronic machines. Very large and bulky, and taking a great deal of time to use for composition, they were programmed by punching holes in a long strip of paper rather like a piano roll. The machine could never be used in a live, or 'real-time', performance because a slight delay occurred before the relay of the composer's role. The RCA machines were, however, very versatile and enabled the composer to programme and connect almost anything. Their range of sounds and effects could not possibly be matched by the smaller machines introduced later.

MOOG SYNTHESIZER Robert Moog developed the first commercial synthesizer in 1964 and in it initiated many features that have since become standard. His synthesizer digitally controlled the voltage – one volt per octave, which became the standard for synthesizers. In 1970 Moog developed the Minimoog, a fully portable monophonic instrument primarily designed for use by rock bands. A number of successors to the Moog synthesizer have developed, providing different features and attributes. These include the Polymoog, invented by David Luce, 1976–1980; the Opus 3, which was a string synthesizer with organ and brass sections; and the guitar-like Liberation.

BYRD-DURRELL SYNTHESIZER Used by the first American rock band to employ electronics extensively in their music: USA, founded in 1967 by Joseph Byrd. Custom built, the synthesizer had ring modulators and echo units controlled by foot pedals.

ROBERT MOOG, PIONEER OF THE COMMERCIAL SYNTHESIZER, DEMONSTRATING A HYBRID ASSEMBLED FROM THE 900 SERIES AND VARIOUS DEVICES.

Ketoff built seven later Synkets, each a modification of the prototype.

Many other portable synthesizers have been made since the Synket. Chief among their users from the late 1960s have been rock bands keen on loud amplification and on generating the many special effects that processed sounds can achieve. Among these groups have been USA, The Mothers of Invention and The Grateful Dead. The event that probably drew most attention to the new technology in the world of popular music was the record *Switched on Bach*, performed on a Moog synthesizer by Walter (later Wendy) Carlos in 1968.

The introduction of digital technology has allowed a further reduction in size. The use of microprocessing enabled the inventors of the Synclavier to make a small portable synthesizer of considerable flexibility. The first model appeared commercially in 1976 and was superseded in 1980 by the Synclavier II. Both were conceived and manufactured at Dartmouth College, New Hampshire and White River Junction, Vermont in New England, USA, by Sydney Alonso, Cameron Jones and Jon Appleton. The Synclavier was followed by several rivals, such as the PPG Wave Computer, the DMX-1000, the AlphaSyntauri and the Soundchaser. But none has the versatility of the two massive, extensively computerized, non-commercial systems – the SSSP at the University of Toronto and the 4X, later the 16X and now being replaced with new defence-industry supported technology, at IRCAM in Paris.

Important Hybrid Synthesizers

AND SYSTEMS

GROOVE – Generated Real-Time Operations on Voltage-Controlled Equipment. Developed by Max Matthews at Bell Telephone Laboratories in 1970.

MUSYS – completed in 1970 by David Cockerell, Peter Grogono and Peter Zinovieff in London.

PDP 15/40 (computer) with EMS 1(synthe-sizing programme) – developed in Stockholm at the Elektronmusikstudion in the early 1970s. It remained in use and oper-ational into the early 1980s when it was dismantled.

SYNCLAVIER – developed at Dartmouth College, New Hamphsire, USA and at White River Junction in 1975. It was the first digital synthesizer and was designed to be an up-market, compact system.

FAIRLIGHT CMI – first manufactured in 1979 in Australia. It possessed two six-octave keyboards, an interactive graphics unit and an alphanumeric keyboard.

DMX-1000 – Digital Music Systems, first appeared in the USA in 1979. Connected to a control computer, such as a PDP 11, it was a programmable computer.

4X – Similar to the DMX 1000 in that it is controlled by a PDP 11 computer, it suc-ceeded early 4A, 4B and 4C models. Notable for its extensive digital signalling processing, it was the first synthesizer used at IRCAM.

SSSP – Structured Sound Synthesis Project, initiated by the University of Toronto, Ontario in 1977 but discontinued in 1983 through lack of funding.

MIDI – Musical Instrument Digital Interface. The first version (Version 1.0) was produced in 1983, and was almost immediately incor-porated by most synthesizer manufacturers as an invaluable component.

CASIO VL-1 – the first miniature all-digital synthesizer aimed at the domestic rather than the professional or institutional mar-ket. It appeared in 1981.

DX – this series of compact, portable syn-thesizers, incorporating the MIDI system, began appearing in 1983. In 1985 the DX7 Mark II was launched with increased timbral potential.

FOUNDED BY TWO STUDENTS OF IMPROVISED MUSIC, GERMAN ROCK GROUP KRAFTWERK USE SYNTHESIZ-ERS, TAPE RECORDERS AND COMPUTERS TO CREATE THEIR MINIMALIST COMPOSI-TIONS. ACCORDING TO KRAFTWERK CO-FOUNDER RALF HUTTER, "TECHNOL-OGY AND EMOTION CAN JOIN HANDS".

COMPUTER MUSIC

THE COMPUTER, ONE of the most remarkable inventions of the 20th century, has had an important effect on the development of music. The rapid advance of computers in the 1990s has produced programmes for writing music down. The traditional method, with pen and paper, was a skill requiring a long time to both learn and execute. Now there are a number of computer programmes that can, for example, replace writing out music for orchestral symphonies or songs with piano accompaniment, with quasi-printed copies; notable is the Sibelius 7. The invention of the synthesizer has also made it possible to link a computer to a keyboard and convert what is played into written symbols. This is achieved by an interface between the keyboard and a computer, the most celebrated being the MIDI (Musical Instrument Digital Interface) (1983).

More radical are the programmes that enable relatively untrained musicians to 'compose'. On electronic keyboards, for instance, a player need play only a simple single melody to be provided with rhythm backing and simple harmonization, each of which has been pre-programmed into the instrument. Such programming has been vastly extended recently, allowing composers to interact with the material to a much greater degree. Musical sounds can now be simulated with greater accuracy and combined to create even orchestral effects by the scientific sampling of the ingredients of complexes of sounds. The effect of this process has been felt in a wide spectrum of applications, from film composers trying out their full orchestral scores in

THE INCREASING COMPLEXITY OF HIS MUSICAL IDEAS LED XENAKIS TO USE A COMPUTER TO HELP ORGANIZE THEM.

their studios (thus saving enormous amounts of time and money in making alterations to scores while live musicians wait to play new material) to large computerized church organs that can simulate the sounds of organs from a wide range of ages, builders and countries.

Computers can be used to help composers select their notes. Some aspects of musical composition have become possible only through the use of computers. Highly complex rhythms and com-

binations of rhythms can be realized exactly through computerization, as can genuinely random choice. A computer can also transform given sounds in a programmed way, as did Henze in his massive work, *Tristan* (1974).

Computers have also been used to 'compose' music. This has been done by programming the computer with a selection of data and criteria for its choices. In the 1950s at Harvard University, F. B. Brooks produced some computer-generated hymn-tunes, and in 1956 Lejaren Hiller and Leonard Isaacson managed to get a computer to write a string quartet, which they called *Illiac Suite*. Each of the movements of this suite were intended to mimic the style of a variety of composers, ranging from Bach to Bartók. Perhaps with more originality and ingenuity, Xenakis composed his *ST/4* (1956–62) for string quartet with the help of calculations made on a computer. Xenakis has described the music resulting from his computer-programmed works as 'stochastic music'.

Getting a computer to make the sophisticated choices needed for composing requires a great deal of painstaking analysis of musical models, as well as intricate scientific know-how to perfect the inputs that create the sounds. The limited amount of music composed by computer probably reflects the time and energy this involves. However, the monumental researches of IRCAM and the imaginative use composers have made of pre-performance preparations and 'real-time' interactions suggest that it is only a matter of time before computers became an even-more active ingredient in the composition of music.

INDEX
PERCUSSION & ELECTRONIC INSTRUMENTS

Percussion and Electronic Instruments

The publishers would like to thank the following sources for their kind permission to reproduce the pictures in this book:

AKG London, Bonani, The Bridgeman Art Library, Camera Press Ltd., Corbis
Mary Evans Picture Library/Agy, Hulton Getty, IMG artists, Lebrecht Collection/Betty Freeman, Luckhurst, London Features International/Ilpo Musto, Mirror Syndication International, Popperfoto, Premier Percussion Ltd., Science and Society Picture Library, University of Edinburgh/Collection of Historic Musical Instruments, Courtesy Yamaha

Every effort has been made to acknowledge correctly and contact the source and/or copyright holder of each picture, and Carlton Books Limited apologises for any unintentional errors or omissions which will be corrected in future editions of this book.

About the Author

Robert Dearling is a respected classical music writer and reviewer. In addition to being a specialist in the music of the 18th century, he has considerable knowledge of musical instruments and over the past 30 years has amassed a huge database of information pertaining to the histories and uses of the world's instruments. He has a wide knowledge of music journalism and has written for many periodicals. He has also written over 400 sleeve and CD booklet notes for among others, Decca, EMI, RCA and Sony. His books include *The Guinness Book of Music*, *The Guinness Book of Recorded Sound*, and *Mozart – The Symphonies*.